benetton

A True Story

Francesco della Barba

LOUDHAILER BOOKS

This first edition published in 2023 by:

Loudhailer Books
13 Lyminster Avenue
Brighton
BN1 8JL

www.loudhailerbooks.com

Contents

Introduction

The purpose of this book is to tell one true story of many events that took place over more than two decades.

Some of these events are funny, some are dreadful, some are important, some less so. But all of them are based on direct experience and represent a fact of life in relation to the people and companies involved.

There have been other stories told about Benetton, both the people and the brand. They have been officially endorsed by the Benetton family.

This is not.

1

Luciano Benetton,
A Life-Changing Encounter

It was 1980 and I was at a turning point in my life.

I was thirty years old, having graduated in economics from the University of Venice. I had had some professional experience in the fashion business, which I liked and where I had many friends.

Having worked for five years in the business, and having started my own company as well, I was now experiencing some difficulties in keeping my business going, in years when there was double-digit inflation, and it wasn't easy to get paid by clients.

When my partners and I eventually decided to shut it down, I ended up going to my CPA accountant in Treviso and asked him if I could go to his firm to be trained as a CPA until I eventually passed my Italian *esame di Stato* (the state certification exam) and officially become a *commercialista* (a CPA accountant).

He gave me a fatherly look and then, smiling, said, "If there is a person who I cannot imagine making a good CPA, it's you! You are too dynamic, too interested in marketing and business events, and you don't have the patience and dedication for a methodical job like mine. Instead, I have one of my clients who, in my opinion, could be the perfect person to have you as his personal assistant, as he's currently involved in a potentially very significant expansion of his business outside Italy, in Europe and, perhaps, the world. His name is Luciano Benetton, and he is the founder of the Benetton fashion business. Do you know him?"

"No," I answered. "I know his brother, Carlo, since we both follow the Treviso rugby team. I met him through some common friends; he is a nice guy."

"Ok then," he said. "I'll arrange for a meeting with Luciano and introduce you to him, and we'll see what comes out of it."

I would have never guessed that this meeting would change my life forever.

Luciano was 45 at that time, and I was 30, so we were both relatively young and very active.

I vaguely knew his story: he was the eldest of four siblings and had been working as a salesman in a men's clothing store in Treviso.

He'd gone on holiday to Scotland a few years earlier, and happened to pay a visit, along with some friends who'd organised the trip, to a small, local factory that was making cashmere sweaters.

He was immediately fascinated by the fact that they were dyeing the garments in tanks, by hand, and beating the garments with a wooden stick to make them softer during the process of dyeing in any particular colour.

He rightly thought that, if he could apply such a method to the manufacturing of classic lambswool sweaters in his region of Italy, it would create a revolution!

At that time, in the store where he worked, he was only selling the classic colours typically available from manufacturers: blue, beige, Bordeaux, forest green, grey and black.

How wonderful would it be to present a men's sweater in light pink, light blue, yellow, red or emerald green, and so on? When he arrived in Treviso, after the trip, he immediately started, with his sister Giuliana, hunting around the dyeing factories in the area if there was any such possibility.

It was a desperate attempt but, with a bit of luck and stubborn determination, he succeeded. He started to make the first few jumpers, hand-made by his sister and a few girls that would help, without a proper factory and warehouse.

He decided he had to try to sell his garments in Rome, the Italian capital, where he would make his product recognizable, but he didn't know anybody, beyond the names of the most famous retailers.

He had heard these names from the suppliers coming to the store where he worked, proudly showing off the names of the big stores in Rome where their products were on sale!

He had a small Fiat 500 back then, which he stuffed with his sweaters, then off he went to Rome, determined to sleep in his car if necessary, and not to come back until he had sold all his sweaters.

His theory was that if the owner of a shop heard there was an unknown guy waiting to see him, who'd been there since the day before, he would think that this guy had to be very confident in his product, otherwise would have already gone away. So, out of curiosity, the owner would eventually, sooner or later, have to see him, and that would be it! He was certain he would make the sale!

This theory worked out well, and soon he was able to leave his job in the men's store in Treviso and start up a new operation with Giuliana in 1963. Their first brand was not called 'Benetton' (he felt it was too arrogant to use their own family name), so they chose 'Très Jolie'! It sounds naïve now, but it was the best they could think of back then. The company was only renamed 'Benetton' in 1965, when Giacometti created the famous original logo, starting from a knitting point that was called *il folpetto* (in Venetian dialect, it means 'the little octopus', which is what the logo resembles).

Let's go back to our first meeting.

It was arranged by my friend the CPA, but he wasn't in attendance, so I met with Luciano by myself.

He was a good-looking guy, but he had something in his eyes that hit me: his general attitude was very nice and relaxed, but his eyes were cold, I would say 'icy'. I thought, *This guy could be dangerous.*

Regardless, the interview went well and, after assessing that his company was starting to expand in Europe, and that I spoke fluent English (which he didn't, by the way), he suggested I go to London for a trial period, where he had already established the Benetton UK office.

"But," he added, "since we operate with a precise marketing and selling scheme, it's very important you understand it and familiarise yourself with it, so I would suggest you spend the next couple of months going around some of our shops in Northern Italy. I will put you in touch with the right person, I'll ask my secretary to call you and give you the details." After agreeing to all this, we shook hands and I left.

A few days later, I started my training period in a store in Verona. I then went on to Bergamo and Brescia, and finally to Milan. This lasted for almost three months, but at the end of the first month, I was going through a deep crisis. One evening, alone in my hotel room, I was trying to focus and understand what the hell was going on. Despite all my credentials and experience, Luciano had put me under the control and instructions of young store managers, who were mostly young girls, who were supposed to teach me how to deal with window-dressing, interior merchandising and display, and selling techniques. So at thirty years old, with a degree in economics, and after having been commercial director of two quite important fashion groups in Italy, I had to swallow the fact that a twenty-year-old girl would nervously knock over the pile of sweaters that I had supposedly "not properly folded and positioned on the shelf"! Then, she would nastily add, "Re-do it, and quickly. I have to close the store!"

It was all so ridiculous, and I was ready to go to Luciano and say, "If you think I need to spend three months folding sweaters and cleaning a store window, maybe we don't see things the same way, and I'll go, thank you very much!"

But of course, that didn't make sense either. Luciano had proven himself to be a smart guy, but this would have been the attitude of an idiot!

What was the explanation for all this frustrating series of events? I asked myself, while crying nervously and holding my head in my hands.

And then it suddenly hit me: Luciano was a man from humble origins. He hadn't had the time and privilege for studying; he'd had to work since he was very young to support his family after his father suddenly died, so he probably regarded the so-called 'managers' as a bunch of spoiled brats who would not be able to make it past the first serious obstacle in life.

So this was clearly a test: had I given up and rejected this stupid training period, I would have shown myself to have no character, and confirmed myself to be one of those arrogant university-bred so-called managers!

Suddenly, I felt my strength increase by hundred. I pretended everything was going well and fascinating, although I'm sure that he understood, between the lines, that I had voluntarily played the role he expected me to play.

It was probably the first example of Luciano's appreciation of my qualities.

He also really liked the fact that I came back having only charged very reasonable company expenses. During my training period, I was of course entitled to a daily allowance for food and beverages, but I did not go to any restaurants for expensive meals. I had always used local *trattorie* or snack bars for quick breaks.

That's when I first heard that Luciano was not a big spender. On the contrary, he was very frugal. I heard a funny story, some years later, from Marina, his girlfriend, who was joking about his parsimony.

They were living at that time in a big villa outside Treviso, where Luciano had a domestic helper, an old lady who had been with him for a number of years, and who was a *tuttofare* (handywoman), because Luciano did not want to employ anybody else.

Luciano wanted her to be his chef, cleaning lady and gardener. The poor woman did the best she could, as she was very attached to Luciano, and didn't want to leave her job.

One evening, he announced they had six guests coming for dinner. He told this lady, "There will be eight of us tonight for dinner, so please prepare that wonderful chicken with potatoes you cook in the oven."

She asked, "Shall I buy two chickens, then?"

"No, I think one is enough," Luciano answered.

"Fine, Mr. Luciano."

She didn't know how to serve one (!) chicken for eight people, so she cut it into small pieces and cooked twice as many potatoes as she would normally do. She then prepared a big serving dish in the centre of the table, that looked big enough for everybody.

Of course, as is usually the case, the guests were very careful not to serve themselves too much, and so by the end of the meal, there was still one piece of chicken with a few potatoes left in the serving dish. Luciano, just before going to bed, remarked to his housekeeper, "Did you see? It's a good job we didn't buy two chickens," pointing at the piece left in the dish. "One was enough, as you can see."

Going back to my feeling of Luciano being an icy guy, I can just point to the fact that years later, in the late 1990s, when Benetton was starting to have some problems, most of his siblings' sons and daughters were already working for Benetton, and this had created some friction with the management, because they were acting more like owners than managers, expressing personal opinions, rather than trying to justify rational marketing strategies, and thus creating confusion.

The four founders got together and bravely decided that it would be better to get all their children out of the way, for the sake of the company they had created.

Each of them had to communicate this decision to their own children, somehow.

Mauro, the son of Luciano, who was officially marketing director of Benetton, was told by his secretary about the decision, and asked to empty his office within the next few days.

Annoyed by the fact that his father didn't even call him to personally notify him of the decision, he ignored the request.

He arrived at work the following Monday morning, said "Hi" to his secretary, and opened the door of his office.

To his bewilderment, his office was completely empty! No furniture, no files, none of his personal belongings, everything had disappeared!

He went back and asked his secretary, angrily, "What the hell happened to all my stuff?"

With a certain embarrassment, she answered, "Mauro, your father gave me instructions to remove everything from your office and to let you know that, from this morning, you no longer work for Benetton Group Spa."

2

My Parents:
an Angel and a Psycho

I was born in Conegliano, a beautiful village on the northern hills of Treviso, a town near Venice.

My parents came from two middle-class families, typical of the hard-working North-East of Italy, considered as the major driving force of the country.

My mother Regina was the second of three siblings, with an older brother and a younger sister. She grew up in Ponte della Priula, an even smaller village, where her father was a prominent figure. My grandfather Carlo was one of the very early pilots during the First World War, together with the national hero Francesco Baracca. He was discharged with the rank of colonel and subsequently became, under the Fascist system, the local *podestà*. In those years of reconstruction after the First World War, agriculture was a key market, and he started to import machinery of various types (tractors, harvesters, etc.) and build some of his own, like silos for cereals storage.

His company grew steadily and started exporting as well into other countries, particularly Brazil and South America.

He was a good person, well respected, and honoured within his community for his contributions to the local council, and so on.

He knew how to be funny as well, with a good sense of self-criticism: I remember when he came to eat at our restaurant *3 Panoce* (3 cobs). My brother and I, and all the staff, wanted to try on his hat, which was very big, I would say HUGE. We would laugh, looking at each other with his hat barely blocked by our ears, such was the size of it!

I also found out, later on, that he liked women too, although very discretely, and he was found, in his last few years, carrying some hosiery for ladies in his briefcase, just in case…

My grandmother, his wife, was very religious and dedicated to the family, and insisted, of course, that her daughter Regina would go to a Catholic college in Treviso, called Le Canossiane, being a high school run by the papal order of nuns since 1810.

My father Eugenio, who was called 'Nino', was the only child of Francesco, my grandfather, and his wife Gina.

Francesco was an enologist, teacher at the local *scuola enologica*, the first of its kind in Italy back in the 1870s, and a farmer and winemaker, with a beautiful winery in Tuscany.

I never met my grandfather. He died of a heart attack at only 49 years of age, just one year before I came into the world.

But my understanding was, during my adolescence, that his best quality was to have left a very good inheritance to Nino, my father, who was suffering from a rare syndrome, the *sindrome del Martello* (the 'hammer syndrome'), as one of his friends jokingly called my father's peculiar repulsion for any object that would, somehow, recall a 'working instrument'!

Nino was never really interested in any kind of job or work activity, he preferred everything else, from women to cars, from poetry to jazz and classical music, from acting to being an amateur comedian for his friends (he had a notebook where he would write down, not to forget them, the best jokes he was hearing here and there).

He had published three books with a local Italian publisher: the first two were poetry and short novels (the second was entitled *Tears, Whores and God*), and didn't sell much, also because my father was definitely an *ermetico* poet, following the steps of Quasimodo, Montale and Ungaretti.

But then he decided to write something light and funny, often using the Venetian dialect, as an alternative to the proper Italian language, telling stories of lovers, sex and infidelities, called *Potacessi Trevigiani* (translation: 'Little Dirty Stories in Treviso'). Suddenly, he sold the first 10,000 copies and it had to be reprinted! In the end, common people probably prefer something easy and funny to read, rather than over-elaborate philosophical concepts and events.

He was a person of great culture, having had the time to deeply discover various aspects of life rather than working eight hours a day like any other mortal!

He had one of the best collections of jazz vinyl records in Europe, from the early 78 rpms, to the late 45s and 33s.

He was a great connoisseur of classical music, and one of his best friends was a member of the famous *Sestetto Chigiano*, a group comprised of two violins, two violas and two cellos.

They had a great concert in 1966 at the glorious theatre *La Fenice* in Venice, playing a sextet by Brahms.

My father had decided to take me there and have me directly experience the beauty of the theatre, and of the music played live by the six musicians.

So, one day he told me, "Come on, Francesco, jump in the car!"

I did it in a second.

"I'll take you to my tailor," he said.

"Why?" I asked, "I don't need any suit or jacket, I don't think."

"Yes, you do," he continued, "because you'll be coming with me in two weeks' time to *La Fenice*!"

It was 1966, I was sixteen, and I knew the famous theatre in Venice to be one of the most beautiful in the world, since its opening in 1792. I was very excited at the idea of going there. I asked him, "What for, Dad?"

"You know my friend Mario, the violin professor at the Venice Conservatory, right? He plays in a sextet called *Sestetto Chigiano* and they will be performing a great Brahms sextet shortly at *La Fenice*. I want you to come with me."

I couldn't believe my ears. It was a magical moment with my father, one of the rare ones when the feeling between us was pure and not contaminated by his crazy character, always ready to explode in a sudden drama!

We arrived at the tailor's shop, and he said, "Giorgio, I want you to make the most beautiful tuxedo for my son Francesco, and it has to be with a proper bow tie, not the ready-made one!"

My father had already taught me how to tie a bow tie; I think I was the only one in my age group in the area to be able to do that, as my school friends didn't even know what we were talking about!

We eventually went to the concert, and I thoroughly enjoyed being among all these classy people attending the concert, in their best fashionable dresses and suits.

But the sudden change of behaviour was always behind the door.

When he was in a good mood, he was the best companion you could dream of! All my friends, during our teen years, knew and adored my father, because he was always joking, having fun and offering something to eat or drink, and interested in our sexual development, so much so that he would personally encourage us, introducing us to older beautiful girls in the area, whether they be sales assistants in fashion shops, nurses or hairdressers.

These girls all had one thing in common: a passion for eating and drinking well and having sex!

So, a person might think that I was very lucky, having such a 'friendly' father! Nothing could be more wrong: Nino was a true bipolar (in those days he was classified as 'schizoid', a less negative definition than 'schizophrenic', a psychiatric disease, quite dangerous for surrounding human beings).

He would jump up and down in his general mood for no reason, and act totally unpredictably. When I was a kid, he taught me the principles he considered the basis for anybody to live a proper life: honesty, integrity, respect for others' freedom, and respect for anybody's right to self-determination. He was not an atheist; he declared himself as *a-religioso*, using the privative 'α' of the ancient Greek. In essence, he didn't believe in the value of any religion.

I accepted all these values as correct and important in my own life, having decided, after years of considering and debating the issue, that I could not believe in any religion either.

So, I always judged my father's strong defence of these principles positively, and particularly his integrity in applying them, at his best, every day and with anybody.

But then again, he was also extreme in his teaching methods, whereby he would apply physical punishment as a normal instrument to form us. If we had done anything wrong, let's say coming back late from playing football with friends, he would become a beast, demanding that you yourself would go to pick up the *battipanni* (carpet beater), bring it to him as he waited in your bedroom, give it to him, remove your trousers and lie down on your stomach, waiting for him to beat you a dozen times on your butt. He was systematic in doing this and I think, now, almost a little sadistic.

As an adult and father, although I strongly believe in the value of a firm education, I never applied such measures with my children, I felt that a severe look and the actual application of rules at home was more than enough. I have never touched my daughters in my life.

My father was a lieutenant in the Italian army during the Second World War, and one who thought that being loyal to your country's command was a duty for an honourable man; he would never defect like most of Italians did at that time, transforming overnight from a convinced fascist to a partisan, shooting his own companions from behind a bush.

I, too, consider this a despicable Italian attitude, that shows up in many situations of our history.

The worst side of his character would appear with my mother. He would suddenly become aggressive and violent for no apparent reason, and the argument would degenerate in beating her.

In 1964, I was a fourteen-year-old teenager, already fully formed and with a strong body, coming from a lot of physical activity in different sports: I played tennis, where I was classified in the national standings; I had skied since I was a kid on our beautiful mountains; and I was competing in the discus throw in our track and field college team.

It was then inevitable that one day that summer, when my parents had another ugly fight which we heard downstairs in our restaurant, located in a 17th century villa. I was with our staff of waiters and chefs, when my father came down with a crazed look in his eyes. I rushed upstairs, to find my mother badly beaten and bleeding.

For the first time in my life, I felt I wanted to kill my father.

I rushed downstairs, confronted him, and started punching him all over. Fortunately, our staff stepped in to block me, otherwise I don't know what the outcome could have been. My father left that day, and I didn't see him for over a year and a half, while my parents were separating.

My mother was a gentle, intelligent and elegant woman, a role model for me, who has been lovingly at my side all my life.

She unfortunately fell in love with this unpredictable young man, and she confessed to me, many years later, that, notwithstanding his violence and abuse, she was madly in love with him, and he was able to win her back, time and time again, particularly with his warm sexuality.

On the other end, my father has always denied that he ever truly intended to get married and having a family.

Many years after their separation, he decided he wanted his freedom back, and started proceedings to have his wedding annulled by the religious tribunal of the *Sacra Rota* in Vatican, the highest appellate tribunal of the Catholic Church.

It's a very difficult and complex procedure, which rarely concludes with the annulment, for obvious reasons. He was however able to obtain it, on the grounds that marrying this young woman had been the only way for him to have sex with her.

He never wanted to marry her, and even less to have children.

The tribunal's long examination, after many months, granted him the annulment, and described my father's personality as schizoid.

I didn't have the time to gradually mature and become a man. I was forced, by our family's events, to take the responsibility for dealing with matters much bigger than me, and confront a reality that was, at times, scary and exciting at the same time.

One day, my uncle Adriano, my mother's brother, came to our restaurant in Conegliano, the *Tre Panoce*, to discuss with my father his exit from the business (my parents were separating right at that time).

I was present at the meeting, since I had been involved in the management of the restaurant.

Adriano and his family wanted Nino to assign the property of the restaurant itself to my mother in exchange for separation. The property was the villa of the 17th century, and included about seven acres of agricultural land around it.

Nino said to Adriano, "You are here to dictate to me the conditions of the separation with Regina," and my mother was also present, silently sitting at a corner of the table, "but you are the usual bastard that wants to take advantage of me without giving me anything in exchange!"

Adriano was already turning red in his face, he felt he was an engineer and well respected businessman in the area, and didn't tolerate my father offending him loudly in front of everybody. He said, "Shame on you, Nino! You not only treat my sister with moral and physical abuse, but you offend me and my family after all we did to help you in any way till now! Our patience is over, now you have to leave on our terms, if you want, as you say, to get back your freedom with the annulment of your marriage."

Nino started to raise his voice, which was already deep and scary, and confronted him. "I will be ready not to assign the property to Regina," he said, "but to my sons, Francesco and Alessandro, and only the usufruct to her!" He went on, "But this will put me in a very weak financial position, so I want you to buy also some land that I own in Conegliano which has been recently turned form agricultural to buildable. It's about 20,000 square metres and I will sell it to you for 250 million Italian lira." This was the equivalent, today, of €2.8 million.

Adriano replied, "Nino, as usual you ask much more than the real value in the market. I know that land and is not worth more than 100 million lira (€1.1 million today), take it or leave it!"

At that point, Nino started screaming insults against his wife's entire family and rushed upstairs. My mother understood, and urged her brother to immediately leave with his car, which he did in a rush, just in time to avoid my father coming downstairs with his Beretta calibre 7.65, his pistol that he had from his army days. He starting firing at the departing car of my uncle, with everyone present terrorized by the shots!

In reality, I always felt that he was aiming well above the level of the car, just to scare my uncle, with no intention of hitting him. Nevertheless…

In the meantime, we had the problem of how to manage the restaurant and to check that the operation was financially viable.

While my mother was taking care of the management, her family stepped in and allocated some human resources to supervise and financially control the business.

At that time, I was fifteen and my uncle's accountant asked me to double-check all purchases, since they appeared to be out of control. I got involved into the process of raw material ordering, particularly from the kitchen, where the chef and his assistant were making orders from the various suppliers.

In those years, the 1960s, the meat in particular was a sensitive issue. Nowadays, restaurants buy portions of everything, vacuum-packed, so the cost is strictly under control, but in those years, you had to buy larger parts, or even entire animal (like a lamb or a bullock) and keep them for longer period in a huge walking refrigerator.

During that summer, I was working either as a trainee chef or making coffees. Some Sundays, I had made up to 500 espresso coffees, and that was tiring and hard work, because in those days you had to grind the coffee, put one or two shots and then press them, and all this had to be done quickly, making sure the coffees were called loudly with the table number, so that the waiter in charge would immediately bring them to table, still hot!

In the kitchen, I would be in charge of tossing the pasta, then putting it onto the plates, again loudly calling the table number for the order to go. The head chef, or his assistant, would be the ones to actually cook the pasta, prepare the sauce, and then pass it over to me to simply toss it and serve it.

Of course, I was also witnessing any event going on in the kitchen, a real 'inferno' of its own! First of all, it was very hot (air conditioning was not available then) and chefs had to drink lots of fluids to replace what they lost through sweating. In some cases, I saw some chefs filling a bottle with half water and half white wine, continuing to drink from this 'personal' bottle hidden away, with the result that he would be quite drunk by the end of the service.

One Sunday evening, however, something caught my attention: an order arrived for a 'fillet Stroganoff' and the chef went berserk because we had finished the fillet meat.

I said to his assistant, "Are you sure there is no more fillet in the cell? It seems to me I had seen some in the left corner."

After a quick check, he came back to me and said, "No, we finished it unfortunately. It will arrive tomorrow."

That gave me the information I wanted: the certainty that there was no more tenderloin.

The following day, the butcher came, as usual, to deliver the meat for the week and I was casually in the area, just to observe our two chefs and the butcher unloading all the various supplies from the van, and signing the relevant delivery notes.

Later, in the early afternoon, I went upstairs in our administrative office and checked the signed delivery notes: they were stating that 22 kg of tenderloin had been delivered (approximately 8 fillets of 2.7 kg each) and I was sure we had none left the evening before. I went carefully to the cell, took all the tenderloin, and weighed it: it was only 16.8 kg, with 6 fillets in the cell. Then I checked where the difference could have been, of course it was in a much cheaper category of meat, and I noticed that some 'tail and bones' had been delivered (we were buying bones to make broth and they were the cheapest item from the butcher). I immediately noticed that the declared weight was less than the actual weight by exactly 5.2 kg, the precise difference in the fillets!

The scam was discovered: the butcher was billing us for 'tenderloin' for other parts like 'tail' and 'bones', overpricing the supply, and no doubt paying the chefs some substantial kickback!

The difference in price was the equivalent of €150, that was being split between the butcher and the two chefs. Not a bad amount to receive every week!

The discovery of this scam brought about the justified dismissal of the chefs, and I received my first encouraging recognition!

We eventually ended up letting the restaurant to Giorgio Ongaro, a restaurateur coming from the famous El Toulà in Milan, owned by Alfredo Beltrame.

Alfredo was a great teacher for a bunch of young assistants, like Giorgio, who later followed their own path and almost all of them became successful.

Giorgio Ongaro took the Tre Panoce to the highest standards and it became one of the best-known restaurants in the region. It was also the first one in Veneto to be awarded a Michelin star in 1978.

He continued until 1979, when we sold the property, and I still see him at his fantastic restaurant in Conegliano, A Casa de Giorgio where, at the age of 80, he still explains, very fast, his 'talking menu' to all of his clients, starting from the famous Escargot Bourguignonne prepared with 18 herbs!

I feel attached to him by an almost filial love.

Life went on, and I finished my studies in 1975, getting a degree in economics at the famous *Ca' Foscari* university in Venice. I then started working in the fashion business with a friend of mine, who was a partner in a well-known local business called King's Jeans.

On a personal level, I was getting tired of a life full of parties and women, which was quite normal in this industry, and I was starting to desire a family, and a child. I was twenty-eight at that time, and I felt that it was the right moment, when I met a very young woman, still in high school, who was only eighteen, and the girlfriend of somebody I knew.

We suddenly fell in love and both wanted to have a baby, and this was when I made the worst mistake of my life.

Her father was a local pharmacist and, immediately after it was confirmed that she was pregnant, he invited me to have lunch with him at a well-known restaurant in Treviso.

I was a bit nervous, because I didn't know him very well. He was originally from the south of Italy, with a very conservative mentality, and I wasn't at ease with him.

He tried to convince me that his daughter was immature, and not ready to cope with a pregnancy and having a baby, but I insisted that he was wrong, and we were both determined to create a family, so we would go ahead with it.

I will carry the weight of this misjudgement for the rest of my life, since what happened afterwards was tragic.

I was commuting from Treviso to Padua every day, and she started to become impatient and nervous, even smoking during the pregnancy, which was, of course, dangerous, and strongly opposed by her gynaecologist.

We soon discovered that she was pregnant with twins, and this further complicated things; she started to feel overwhelmed with the development of events.

Our twins were born premature and needed a couple of weeks in the incubator, but her behaviour worsened, as she refused to wake up at night to feed them. So I ended up doing that myself, twice a night, and with double time, since I had to feed two boys, not one, and then go to work early in the morning.

Although our families did their best to help with managing this, the situation quickly degenerated into furious fights and arguments during the night and, within a year, in separation.

The real tragedy had yet to unfold: only when the boys were two and a half, being declared since the beginning as 'prematurely born' and therefore normally slower than other babies to reach a normal level of growth, I realized that they were not pronouncing even a single word, and this made me very suspicious and worried.

I ended up taking them to a famous US neurologist who came to nearby Vicenza twice a year for consultations. After a few quick tests, he discovered that the diagnosis was terrible: severe brain damage due to lack of oxygen at the birth or during pregnancy.

My boys would be disabled for the rest of their lives.

I was shocked when he told me the reality of the situation. I reacted by losing my patience, swearing at destiny, God, the doctors, and smashing up a couple of objects in the medical studio we were in.

The American neurologist was very patient and understanding. He quietly told me, "Even if I could magically answer your questions about how, when and why all this happened, would it change the future of your kids?"

This simple affirmation froze the blood in my veins, and I was overcome by a great sadness, I apologized to him, and started to think about what to do next.

I had two choices: either die with my sons, maybe jumping off a bridge with them, or accept that the best I could do was to take care of them for the rest of their lives and go on with my own.

I chose the second option, and saved myself.

3

The Early Days, King's Jeans, Americanino and Kamikaze

After graduating from the University of Venice in 1976, I started to work with a fashion company called King's Jeans in Northern Italy. At that time, I wasn't particularly interested in fashion, and my choice came about because of my friendship with one of the principals.

Like many other young Italians during the seventies, I was looking for an opportunity to start my career in a more dynamic and informal company. The typical destination, after studying marketing and accountancy in the equivalent of business administration courses, was to go to a bank, a big company, or a firm of *commercialisti*, the Italian equivalent of certified public accountants.

Fortunately, one of my dear friends was the younger brother of Rossella Goldsmith. She had founded, with her husband Adriano, a small manufacturer of jeans near Vicenza, in the now very famous north-east of Italy, called King's Jeans.

This small company was producing and selling mainly jeans and other casual clothes, and was sub-contracting the production to local workshops, to avoid both taxes and local union control.

Italy was going through a very difficult period, with political and economic struggles. The left parties, Communist, Socialist and others, were greatly influencing social life and industrial relations. Big companies like Fiat were suffering from long and costly strikes and insufficient productivity. To avoid all this, King's Jeans was diversifying its sources of production by appointing small, family-owned workshops. These were employing a maximum of fourteen people each, since this was the level under which, by law, unions had no power of enforcing the National Labor Contracts.

Another important aspect of all this industry was the so-called *nero* (literally 'black money'), meaning the fact that a firm would not invoice all its sales and accordingly record them in its books. It would simply deliver goods on a 'cash basis', and no trace of the delivery would remain between the two parties, thus originating the *nero* revenue that would ultimately not be taxable as part of official profits.

I remember reading a report by the Wall Street Journal, a few years later, about the so-called 'hidden economy' in Italy. It described how this was a very important element of stability of the country because it was diverting taxpayers' money that would have been otherwise dispersed in the corrupt public administration that was causing so many problems to the country in those years.

Nothing could have been more correct than this. In fact, many small industrialists and artisans were secretly investing their *nero* in real estate or in their own companies, or even in public bonds, pushing forward the private sector. It is ironic that the Italian state offered higher interest than bank deposits, becoming a competitor for the private sector in attracting savings with the incredible incentive that the interest was tax-free! Capital gains tax was still an unknown concept in Italy in those years and was considered as *blaspheme* by any private investor.

Somebody once told me that Italy had only one, albeit important, difference from the South American states which were so depressed and unstable with very high inflation: the smart Italian politicians had chosen not to borrow money from sources like the International Monetary Fund, but directly from their own compatriots. It was like asking your brother for a temporary loan, instead of the bank! If your brother has some money to give you, it will be much more difficult and less stressful if he asks you for his money back, and it will certainly not cost you the repossession of your house!

Going back to King's Jeans, it was a lot of fun to participate in a company were everything was done with a feeling of trust and family relations.

The company was so successful in those early years, that we had retailers queuing in front of our warehouse since early morning, to make sure that they would get their daily delivery of goods, like normal people in front of a bakery waiting for fresh bread.

The sales reps, called *agenti* in Italy, had the responsibility of going around in different areas to promote the sales of new styles. We did not, back then, create a seasonal collection, but rather we'd propose new styles every few weeks, to respond to the volatile fashion market in the fastest way.

To do so, the *agenti* had expenses to sustain and needed cash. There was a shoebox in the middle of the warehouse, with a split on top where we would drop the cash coming in from the proceeds of selling the goods.

Some agent would loudly shout to Rossella or to Gegè, her brother, that he needed some cash to go to Milan and see a client, and so he would take it from the box. There was no record, no receipt, and no proof of purchase when he came back.

King's Jeans didn't last much longer with this kind of 'friendly' administration, and the owners split their ways and were forced to sell to a rich local entrepreneur.

His name was Nereo Bressan and he had made his fortune through political connections in Vicenza. He owned a small factory making iron and steel products, then made a big advance when there was suddenly a new highway to be built in the region.

This motorway, that connected Vicenza to some northern locations where nobody really needed to go, became famous as the 'Bi-Ru-Pi', a nickname coming from the initials of the three local politicians elected as members of parliament in Italy: Bisaglia, Rumor e Piccoli. They were all members of the Christian Democrats, the most popular party in Veneto region at the time, and they were as corrupted as anybody else was.

Nereo managed to get granted the contract for manufacturing all the guardrails for the new motorway, and he made millions.

He was suddenly a *nouveau riche*, and took pleasure in blowing his money like crazy, for anything he liked. Since nobody knew him in society for his manufacture of unglamorous guardrails, he decided to buy out King's Jeans, which was in financial difficulty, to gain social connections and all the beautiful girls that traditionally circle around in the fashion world.

Gegè went on to form another company, called Americanino, to compete with King's Jeans, and I would eventually end up working with him there a few months later.

In the meantime, I had my duty as marketing director for King's and had to deal with the company's financial troubles, involving several banks, and unions.

During a hectic meeting with unions and our representatives, I received a call in the room and angrily picked up the phone. "I told you I was not to be disturbed!" I almost screamed to my secretary.

"Well, sorry, it's Nereo on the line for you!"

He was the only person I had to answer to!

"Get ready," he said. "I'll come and pick you up in 45 minutes. We'll go to Viareggio and try the boat of Bonomi, the offshore world champion! It's a fantastic, super-fast powerboat, and he might sell it to me!"

"Nereo," I said calmly, "I'm in the middle of a very hectic meeting with union representatives, our agents and our CFO. I really cannot leave it!"

He immediately went on with his acute voice, "I don't give a shit, send the unions to hell and get ready!"

"Nereo, it would not only be a very bad decision for your company, but it's also physically impossible for me to leave, downstairs the workers have organized pickets and are blocking all entrances!"

At this point, he exploded. "I'll come with my helicopter and land on the roof in twenty minutes. If you are not ready, you are fired!"

I wasn't sure that he would have fired me, but it was his way of saying that he wanted me to be with him in something he enjoyed more than the business problem I had to fix for him! It was the typical behaviour of an Italian self-made businessman, who had gone from being poor and humble, to rich and arrogant.

Reluctantly, I went along with his plan. We flew with his private jet (one of the very few early ones in Italy, it was 1977) to Viareggio, drinking champagne during the trip.

He was a good companion, but could not handle his alcohol, and would inevitably get drunk after two or three glasses, then become very bizarre.

He insisted he wanted to try to personally pilot the powerboat, and almost killed us all with a sudden manoeuvre that nearly threw him out of the boat at high speed. Luckily, he was hit on his right arm, and this quietened him down.

When we flew back to Vicenza, we went, with some nice girls that had been with us all the time, for a last drink in a famous central bar where all the *Vicenza bene*, the high society in town, would gather for an *aperitivo*.

He complained to the owner behind the bar that the wine served to us, contained in old barrels behind the counter, was of poor quality.

"Piero," he said with the pronunciation of a drunk, "this wine you gave us is really bad!"

"Come on, Nereo, what do you mean? It's a very nice Valpolicella Superiore I personally chose from a small producer near Verona and that we aged in these oak barrels for eighteen months!"

Nereo didn't really understand anything about wine; he had no sense of smelling aromas and no educated palate to recognize the complexity of a good red wine, but he wanted to be seen as someone competent.

He turned to me and another friend there and asked, "What do you think?"

We both laughed, amused, and said, "Come on, Nereo, since when are you a wine connoisseur? This is an excellent Valpolicella!"

We dared expose him to criticism in public and he couldn't accept it, as drunk as he already was, and in response pulled out his gun, a Smith-Wesson P38, which he always had with him, and shot all the wine barrels, while everybody dived to the floor, screaming!

Anybody else would have been arrested for something like this, but he was a friend of the *questore*, the local police chief, so nothing happened to him.

With such a boss, it was time for me to move on. I soon joined Gegè at the new Americanino headquarter, which was in an area full of these workshops, in a very flat part of the *Pianura Padana*. The nearest village was Cavarzere, where everybody knew everybody.

Gegè had little money to start this new adventure, and needed a strong financial partner. He decided to propose the deal to a guy called Bardelle. His story was amazing: he was the driver of the local Piove di Sacco (another small local village) ambulance, but, ambitious and smart as he was, he soon realized that there was a better future in the textile manufacturing business.

He had met a local girl, whose family were already wealthy enough to own a few workshops, although working for the traditional industry of men's clothing, like San Remo and Lebole. He married the girl, certainly not for her attractiveness, but for the money, and for her quality as a hard worker. He then convinced her family to abandon the traditional sector and start working as sub-contractors for the new jeans industry.

His wife was known to her employees as the *carabiniere*, which is the name of a very famous police force in Italy, for her toughness in forcing the girls, without any extra pay, to stay for one or even two hours more at the end of the working day.

She would force them to make the repairs she deemed necessary: a wrongly sewed pocket or sleeve, or any other imperfection she might have spotted.

Bardelle was a very rough guy; the perfect example of the poor, uneducated person suddenly arrived at unthinkable levels of richness.

He was spending money in a showy way that was insulting even for his most loyal employees: he had a line of sport cars and bikes, worth a fortune, parked out the front of the office. He was proud of remarking that for every pair of jeans he made, his 'black' profit was $1.

Everybody knew that his six workshops were producing some 2,500 pairs a day, which meant his daily profit was $2,500, net of taxes, because he wouldn't almost pay any!

My salary at that time was approximately $700 a month, so you can imagine how much we liked this guy! However, he was the only partner for Gegè, and he had already established his own label, with a very basic product, distributed mainly in Germany and called 'Outsider'.

Americanino became the other one, and so we started with the target of expanding mainly in Italy, where Outsider was barely known.

The business flourished, and soon we were manufacturing and shipping 25,000 to 30,000 garments a week. In this scenario, finding the 'right' fabric, in terms of weight and colour, was very tough, since there was no planning in advance.

We then relied on the textile industry of Prato, a town near Florence, already famous for these 'pirates' of the textile industry who were incredibly fast and smart. Did you need 50,000 metres of a certain coloured 'drill' to manufacture a classic five-pocket style? They would be there a couple of days later, in the required quantities, as long as you didn't argue too much about the quality (never the best), or price (always the worst), and you were ready to pay cash on delivery.

Between the various agents, there was also a young and aggressively ambitious one, called Alberto Biani, who soon realized that there was a potential for a brand targeting the wealthier and more fashion-conscious young consumers, who still wouldn't choose, or be able to afford, to go to the best-known designer brands.

He pushed us to create a new label by the name of New York. He became a well know designer on his own, with the label Alberto Biani in Europe and America. He is a wonderful guy, full of life, with a taste for gambling.

That early world of casual fashion was really a factory of young brains that would one day prove their own strength and creativity.

A simple example is the extraordinary success of a man like Renzo Rosso, the founder of Diesel, a worldwide known jeans label, who was at that time the young warehouse stock-keeper of Americanino!

He is now very wealthy and, although undoubtedly a very intelligent guy, he still has the ancient fear of poverty, typical of poor people that had to fight their own way to success.

He was at dinner one day with some mutual friends when, very proudly, he told the story about how his son had organized a party for about 400 friends, at his own villa, inviting them all during a summer evening.

To their surprise, the kids found out that, although everything was beautifully prepared, with a swimming pool and music available, drinks were to be charged at $2 each, like they were at a disco!

In this way, the proud father said, his son made a profit that allowed him to go on vacation with some friends.

In the father's eyes, his kid showed a business acumen that was very promising.

In my eyes, they are a bunch of mediocre, stingy people that can only see money, and not the pleasure of inviting your own friends, since you are one of the few that can afford it!

I would have kicked my son in the ass for a week, if he pulled a stunt like this, but people have different views, and that's life.

In this sense, Luciano Benetton is very similar, since he does not like to spend any money at all, particularly if it comes out of his own pocket.

It is funny that I started to hear about Benetton in those early years, the mid-seventies, when the brand was purely considered a sweater manufacturer and, in the young fashion industry, was certainly not perceived as a potential major rival or competitor.

Gegè was saying, at that time, "Who is this Benetton? He only makes a few cheap jumpers; he has no sense of creativity and will never be a threat to us!"

Never was such a judgment more wrong, for ten years later Americanino was on the verge of bankruptcy, and Benetton was considered a potential buyer of the group, and its only hope of survival. Benetton eventually decided not to buy, and as a result Americanino went down the drain, with over $70 million of debts. Gegè has still to recover from that shock in his life.

Gegè had some brilliant intuitions, and one was that we needed to coordinate better the creative part of our job: design of styles and research on fabrics was unified under one roof in a new company, called Dress Idea, that would also work as a consultant for others.

One thing that amazed me was that we were buying fabrics presented and commercialized with technical descriptions such as: height 140 cm, weight 620 gr., price x per metre, and so on.

But nobody was ever checking on the correctness of this information. I started to question why we had to pay a certain price per metre, if the weight of the fabric was 20% lower than declared and therefore, having less cotton in it, should have been less expensive to buy. I was successful in many situations in reducing our purchase price, after having received our deliveries, and thus adding additional unexpected profit to our operation.

While Americanino was becoming stronger and our sales were steadily growing, we started to have a problem with our main designers. They were twins, Alberto and Alessandro Cacciavillani, originally from a small town near Rome.

Their myth was Kenzo, and their style was greatly influenced by the famous Japanese. They were becoming increasingly frustrated by the fact that they had to design a very commercial product and felt that their own creativity was somehow contained and suppressed.

I spoke to Gegè and told him that we were better off forming a small new company to let them express their own instincts and so we did, giving them 50% for free.

The other shares were equally split between Gegè and me.

The name was Kamikaze, of course chosen by Cacciavillani. We started making crazy outfits in very small numbers, at expensive prices.

We rented another office in the vicinity, which worked as warehouse as well, from where we would cut the materials, send them out for manufacturing, collect them after being ironed and finished, and finally ship them out.

In the beginning, this was somehow exciting and fun.

I remember staying until late at night with the electric cutters to manually cut the layers of fabric: it was almost like artists creating their own product.

A year later, we had had some success in introducing the label in some of the best Italian shops dealing with the new fashion offerings for the younger audience.

This was 1978, when many designers, who are now famous, had still to come around, like Dolce & Gabbana, Moschino, Romeo Gigli, and others. Some fashion magazines started to give us some attention and publish editorials, to our great satisfaction.

One week in 1978, the monthly magazine *Amica* gave us the front cover, with a photo of a Kamikaze evening dress.

This was the peak of our exposure, but we were still making few items and our turnover was at the lowest levels.

I then received a call from the Fiorucci's office in Milan, with Elio Fiorucci on the line, telling me that he had seen our product and would like to introduce it in his shops.

It was a big step forward. Full of hope, we left for Milan with our collection.

After briefly meeting Elio, a very pleasant man whom I would know much better years later, we continued with a couple of his buyers.

They were not very interested, of course because they were being forced, by his judgement, to buy from us, so they started to quickly look through the styles, with a snobby attitude that really frustrated us.

At the end, they chose only three samples, and refused to increase the selection when we told them that it was too small and not representative of our overall look.

I suddenly told them to get lost, packed our collection and left. This episode gave me the clear view that it was now time to either capitalize on our growing name, or we would remain insignificant forever.

The following spring/summer collection, I believe it was in 1979, we had a beautiful new fabric, a 'cotton satin' that looked like a 'raso', developed by Cacciavillani with one of our suppliers. Raso was normally, at that time, made of synthetic yarns, like rayon or polyester. They had instead created a fabric in pure cotton with a special 'calandratura' (the fabric goes through a system of metal rolls, with temperature and certain humidity, that make it shiny but 'natural', instead of the visible synthetic look of raso).

Being of 100% cotton, it was also possible to make it in delicate pastel colours.

I took the car and personally went all the way to Florence, Rome, Naples, Palermo, Milan, and other towns in two weeks.

The outcome was clear: we had a wonderful material, but it was applied to very fashionable styles of pants and skirts, not easily sellable. Everybody said to me, "I would only buy 30 or 40 pieces in this style, but if you make a more 'normal', 'commercial' one, I will take 500."

At the end of the trip, I had collected the usual small orders, but we had the chance, for the first time, to manufacture 5,000 pants of a style we had to come up with.

Cacciavillani bluntly refused to do so, on the argument that we would devalue the label, by making 'commercial' clothes like many others and that Kamikaze had to remain a very fashionable brand only.

I was so frustrated, so depressed, after all my efforts, in realizing that they were mere dreamers, and would remain so for the rest of their lives.

I decided to quit and go into a different direction. I agreed with Gegè that he would buy me out, and I started to think about what to do next.

4

Benetton in the UK and the Arab Royal Buyers

L et's go back to the first meeting with Luciano.

After my three months of training, I was sent to London, where Benetton had opened the UK headquarters in the King's Road.

The first store opened in London was in Bond Street, an important location regarded as a 'fashion district', somehow similar to what Via Montenapoleone in Milan is.

It wasn't the highest pedestrian traffic (Oxford Street was immensely busier with people everywhere), but if you wanted to be seen by the right customer, you had to be in Bond Street.

The second store was opened in Knightsbridge, just opposite what is now Chanel, on Brompton Rd and Sloane Ave.

It immediately became Luciano's favourite store in the world because it was the perfect emblem of the Benetton concept: a small sale area (500 sq. ft.) with open shelves for the customers to freely touch and try on, and a back-up storage area with the bestselling items available in all sizes.

The small area had been created on purpose, to be easily crowded with people queuing to pay at the cashpoint.

Think about it: if you are looking for a restaurant where to eat in an area you don't know and you don't have any reference, where do you go? Almost certainly to the most crowded one, never in an empty restaurant!

The same psychological approach is applicable in fashion: when you see a busy store, with people queuing, you want to go in and see what they are going crazy for!

Well, in Knightsbridge the queue had to be organized and controlled by bobbies (the London police officers) in a line of two that was going around the corner until the beginning of Sloan Avenue, some 3 – 400 yards!

It was unbelievable, hundreds of customers that were buying 10-12 items each, all very colourful and coordinated and, above all, very cheap for those days!

Luciano was proudly mentioning, about this store, that it was selling, in a single year, the entire production of an average Italian knitwear factory: over 100,000 pieces, which meant about 270 tickets every day. A phenomenal success.

I was, one day, in the coffee shop within the Antiques gallery below our office in King's Road and had to order a quick lunch snack. I opted for a 'jacket potato with ham and cheese'. When I received my order, I was reading an Italian newspaper and casually put the fork in the potato, nicely covered with melted cheese, to discover, with horror, that inside there was jam!

When I asked the girl what the hell had she brought me, she candidly answered that I had ordered 'jam and cheese'!

This made me conclude two things: I urgently needed to improve my English accent and knowledge, and I could not expect from English people the same personal interpretation I could find in Italy. In a similar situation, an Italian waitress would have asked me whether I was sick or mad to ask for jam in my potato. The English one thought that it was not her business and that I was free to order what I wanted.

The second episode is related to the very famous English concept of 'good value for money'.

One of the first Benetton operators was Ted, an experienced independent retailer, from Bath, the beautiful town in the west countryside of South England. During the buying in London, we were looking at a nice 'jacquard' jumper (a fantasy one), but he considered the price too high. To explain his view, he said, "Do you know the difference between an Italian and an English? The Italian, having an *aperitivo* with his friends, would make sure that everybody knows that his new Jacket is an Armani one and that he has spent £ 1,000 for it. He would say this with pride and show-off spirit. The English one, having a beer in a pub with a friend that asked him where he bought that nice jacket he was wearing, would answer that he had found it in a local shop selling second-hand clothes and had paid only $ 10 for it. He would say this with the same amount of pride as the Italian one!"

His description of the two different mentalities struck me as an excellent one and still is the best definition I heard of two very different cultures. I would later find out that Americans comprise both: in metropolitan areas they are very similar to the Italians, in the rest of the country they are often like their English cousins.

At that time, I was, of course, going back quite frequently to Italy. During one of these trips, we were out for dinner with some local entrepreneurs, and among them was Giuseppe (known as 'Bepi') Stefanel, the Benetton's main competitor. He had adopted the same strategy to modernize the family's business, which had been a traditional *maglificio* – a factory producing woollen sweaters and accessories in a very classic way, both in terms of shape, fit and colours.

By doing this, while having at his back the potential of industrial production already established, he created a big network of Stefanel stores in Italy, and he was therefore not very well regarded by the Benetton family.

At a certain point, he asked me, quite curious, how had I found the UK in my recent experience, and what were the main differences from Italy.

I started to describe everyday life in the UK, underlining funny traditions (funny for us Italians, but very civilized habits in respect of the community and its social rules). He wanted some examples, which I emphatically told him about (to impress those present) such as queuing, obey the rules when driving a car, and freedom of speech regarding politicians.

I concluded with a metaphor that came out quite effectively, winning Bepi's esteem, as I said, "The UK is a rich country, with very little public deficit, and poor inhabitants. Whereas Italy is a poor country, with a huge public deficit, but made of rich individuals!" And this was very true.

I was still running my original three stores, which were doing well, and occasionally even driving myself a little van to move goods around them.

One day I was driving from Putney to Windsor on the motorway, when, just after the junction at Heathrow Airport, I noticed a huge queue of cars, blocked there by some accident happened further on. The traffic jam was horrendous, and I suddenly realized that I would never make it to the store in time to bring some very fast- selling clothes they needed there.

I immediately pulled left on the emergency lane (in UK, remember, they drive on the left side) and saw that the junction I just passed, 300 hundred yards back, was closed by the police. Being Italian, I decided to try a way out. I put my emergency lights on, and very slowly started to drive in reverse towards the police. I went out of the van and pretended to be an employee of Benetton and that, if I didn't deliver on a busy Saturday the goods to the store, I would be sacked.

The policeman, not at all moved by my story, told me that I was not allowed to drive backwards on motorways and that he could not let me exit there; I had to go on into the traffic jam and wait until the motorway was freed.

This is what I did, saying to myself that, had I been in Italy, the policeman would have probably let me out. What I did not expect at all was that a couple of weeks later, I received a police report with a warning for the offence and two points on my license!

I have always respected the different culture and obedience to laws of the Britons, but I still think that sometimes it becomes ingenuity. It happened to me many times to be driving on a motorway and find a long, very long queue of cars, sometimes two or three miles, and think that there must had been an accident or a traffic jam at the junction, on the exiting lanes. When I reached the junction, I then found out that there was only one lane on the left queuing, while the other was almost free! This is because the English find very attractive to put themselves in line, as soon as they see one, even if they don't need to. We have the same attraction only for women.

On another occasion I was in London, at the beginning of my Benetton experience, waiting for a bus in the West End to go back to the office. It was pouring down rain, and there was a bus shelter divided in two parts, one was for certain bus numbers, let's say 2,3 and 5, and the other for 8, 10 and 12. I was waiting for a bus of the first three, like most of the other people there, who were queueing under the rain, in an individual pretty long line. I thought, *Why do I need to stand in the rain when I can wait comfortably under the other half of the shelter?* So, I stood there, well covered, and when my bus arrived and I tried to jump on it, the people in queue loudly complained with me that I had to stay in queue and blocked me from taking the bus! This was unconceivable for me as an Italian, but I learnt the lesson at my expense!

This fundamental difference between English and Italians has proven itself many times: once I had driven to meet a client in a small town in my area, parked properly and paid in coins at the meter. When I returned, I found a parking ticket that I got for only a couple of minutes of expired parkin term. I was swearing for my bad luck but, once back at the office, I gave the ticket to my secretary to pay. Kim, my loyal and very smart assistant, did so, only to come back to me a week later, to reveal that we had received a letter from the police headquarters. The letter stated that, since their record showed that I had been precise in paying all my tickets timely and this one had been issued only for less than two minutes excess parking, they rewarded my attitude by waving the ticket and returning our check.

I was shocked: this would have never happened in Italy, and I decided to frame the check with the police letter and hang them on the wall to be seen by all the Italians that would eventually visit our office, for them to understand and appreciate the different mentality and respect for collective rules.

On another occasion, during one of my trips back from USA to my English office, I took our company car and drove to Bristol for an urgent matter with a client.

I was driving on a dual carriageway, not a proper motorway, where the speed limit was only 40 m/h, not 70! Immerse in my personal thoughts about the problem, I was driving, in typical Italian fashion, at almost 100 m/h!

I suddenly heard a police siren behind me and realized that a grey car that was following me was actually an unmarked police car! I stopped and the officer asked me my car documents and driving license. When he realized that the car was owned by an English company, but my license was Italian, he informed me that, given the speed at which I was driving, I was under arrest and that I had to be judged immediately at the local magistrates' court.

He drove my car to the destination in Bath and I was in the back of the police car driven by his colleague. When we arrived at the local magistrates' court, I was temporarily locked in a cell, waiting for the first judge to arrive. After half hour, the same officer came to conduct me through and underpass, dark and humid, and I eventually surfaced in a courtroom, inside the defendant's cage!

I felt horrible, I had never thought that one day I would've been in a cage, accused of a criminal act. The judge was a woman, with a severe face, that asked me a few questions and finally informed me that the law prescribed I was arrested to avoid me leaving the country without paying the proper fine and that, had I been an English citizen, my driving license would have been confiscated and suspended for at least six months!

I realized that breaking the speed limit was regarded, in the English society and quite rightly so, as a very important violation putting at risk anybody's else safety and thus severely punished.

In Italy, speed limits are normally entirely and easily disregarded, and the concept of respecting them is far away from Italian drivers.

The judge than unexpectedly asked me how much money I had in my pockets. I immediately realized that she wanted to assess the maximum fine I would be able to pay, to avoid further delays and procedures.

I quickly responded that I had "around 70 or 80 pounds with me" when in fact I was sure I had more than £500!

Sensing that I was probably lying, the judge asked angrily the officer if he had properly searched me at the time of my arrest and he candidly said "No," with an embarrassed expression and his face turned red.

The judge then informed me, angrily, that by law it was now too late to search my pockets and therefore she had to set a fine of £70 that I had to pay immediately to be released with the car.

I understood that she was probably thinking, *This nasty Italian has taken advantage of the naïve approach of our police officer and I only regret I can't give him a much higher fine.*

Another side of the picture on the two countries' good and bad qualities came to my mind a few years later during a business lunch in New York.

I was with Royce Pinkwater, a phenomenal lady, strong and smart, one of the best Real Estate brokers in USA who arrived at the position of executive vice-president of Sotheby's Real Estate and then formed her own corporation and a new concept platform called 'Pinkwater Select'.

We were talking about the recurrent Italian government crisis and the bad economic situation, and she was telling me, to encourage me to see a positive possible outcome, that, "Italians have periodically these severe crises but, given their intelligence and creativity, they are always bouncing back stronger and healthier, and this will happen this time as well!"

I thanked her for her positive and generous appreciation of Italian good qualities, but to make her understand my disbelief that this time it would have been the same story, I suddenly asked her:

"If I'm not wrong, you too have a saying that if you put a rotten apple in a basket of good ones, it will spoil all the others, correct?"

She answered "Yes, we do, and so?"

"Well," I continued, "the situation in Italy is this bad because of the diffused corruption. Corruption is radically instilled in most Italians, and thinking of eradicate it is utopian, like hoping that putting a good apple in a basket of rotten ones will regenerate them all!"

She smiled and told me "This is a very good way to make me understand your point of view!"

For example, I was in Windsor in 1981 where I was going to open the first Benetton store on my own. I was in the unit on High Street with the real estate agent involved and an electrician he introduced me to. The interior decoration was all coming from Italy and the only part of the store I had to arrange in UK was the electric system, because of different voltages used.

At the end of the meeting, after discussing the final price, I said to him "Well, if you want, we can do the usual 50% invoiced and the other 50% in cash, we both save some!" This was typical Italian attitude and I was very surprised when he said to an older guy who was with him at our meeting "Let's go!" and rushed, literally ran out of the store to be never seen again!

I asked to the agent if I had said or done something wrong and, half laughing, he answered, "Of course you did! Proposing an illegal evasion of taxes scared him and he will never be involved with you again!"

That made me think that, in fact, the electrician was right, if you don't respect your duties in the first place, how can you expect that politicians and state employees behave according to the law and not use the same opportunities to enrich themselves? And then we Italians loudly complain that our Government steals public money as if we were somehow different...

You can actually see very clearly this reality, for instance, in airways operations by the two countries: Italy is full of episodes like the one when I arrived, one late afternoon, at the 'Freccia Alata' lounge in JFK airport (the Italian V.I.P. lounge), where the girls working there, were always very nice and available for me, mainly because I was inviting them at the seasonal pre-sale of garments.

We were always organizing these sales to get rid of the samples we had just used for orders of the stores in US, very much appealing to anyone because they were sold at 70/80% discount on the S.R.P.

That day one of them told me that I was regularly booked in business class and asked me if I needed anything, since the flight was overbooked.

I answered that I was fine and complained that I hated these overnight flights where I couldn't sleep because, unless I was on a horizontal bed-type resting surface, I was not able to sleep.

She came back fifteen minutes before boarding and said to me, "You'll be fine! I have blocked on our PC for you a full central row of four seats in the first line of economy class (the airplane was a Jumbo that had a configuration in economy of 2 - 4 - 2 seats aisle to aisle).

"The important thing is that you pull up the armrests in the middle and go to sleep immediately after take-off, because the plane is overbooked and you don't want someone to move to one of your free seats just, maybe, to better watch the movie. Anyway, I have already told my colleague hostess on flight and she will take care of you."

At that moment, I had not realized that, in fact, she was assigning to me three economy seats free of charge in overbooking, therefore leaving on the ground three travellers that could have used those seats and paid for them! And that was practically stealing the equivalent cost of the three seats from Alitalia.

I suddenly realized all this when, feeling very embarrassed and ashamed, I boarded with everybody looking at me and not understanding how I could have been so lucky not to have anyone sitting near me in a central row of four!

I never accepted a similar offer again.

Another time, some hostess in Freccia Alata said to me, "Sorry, you have to fly in economy, although you were regularly booked in business class, but all the business class has been requested and taken away by the Italian Foreign Minister On. De Michelis and his entourage of 30 people."

De Michelis was well known to come for a week and officially attend some political meetings, in reality just having fun for a long week-end with his group of friends, going to clubs and discotheques all night long. I would be very curious to see what was the real cost involved, for the taxpayer's money, in such a trip of 30 people (!), with hotels, discos, restaurants and, of course, flights.

On the contrary, English management of British Airways has always positively surprised me throughout the years.

The most amazing event happened, again at the JFK, one day that I was going to London with my ex-wife, my two daughters and the baby-sitter. We were booked, the four of us, in Business Class, and our baby-sitter in Economy.

We were at the business lounge to check-in and found out that we had, because of overbooking, four different seats spread around. My daughters were seven and two at the time, there was no way we could manage that having a two year-old girl sitting on her own.

I complained with the manager on duty who came back, after a few minutes, with this, "We are very sorry for the trouble, but unfortunately the overbooking has created this horrible situation and we ask you if you would accept to take the Concorde instead."

I almost screamed, "Are you crazy? I have flown the Concorde already and I have paid $4,000 one way, which means I would have to spend $20,000 for the tickets!

At that point I was shocked, as he continued telling me, "No sir, we offer that you take the Concorde for free!

The only problem is that your luggage is already on the other flight, so you'll have to collect it after the arrival.'

"Of course, I don't mind, but you'll have to board our babysitter as well upgrading her from economy."

He looked her dangled upwards and, with a sigh, he said, "Let's go, the Concorde leaves in ten minutes!"

It was a very funny moment when we entered, as last, the Concorde almost full of businessmen who must have thought, *Who the hell is this guy that takes the Concorde with all the family?*

Our babysitter took every removable object that had the Concorde logo on it, even the white towel on the head rest, as a souvenir!

We then arrived at Heathrow six hours before and, instead of meeting Gino at his home in Iver, we went straight to his Santini restaurant where we arrived perfectly in time for dinner. When he saw us coming through the door, he said to me in disbelief, "What are you doing here? What's going on?" and I hugged him and said, "I just wanted to have dinner with you tonight, so I decided to change for the Concorde!"

Knowing the cost of the flight and not imagining that it would be a joke on my side, he continued, "I always thought that Luciano is paying you agents too much in commissions and now you have lost any common sense!"

When I told him what happened, he couldn't believe that

BA had been so smart to fill the empty spaces in the Concorde (ready to take off anyway) and get the full price for normal business seats on the overbooked flight. Just opposite to what Alitalia would have done!

The first experience with the Middle East market was an astonishing one. Benetton sent me the details of the first two entities that expressed interest in opening: Mrs. Al Sabah, from the royal family of Kuwait, and her close friend, the Princess of the Sultanate of Oman.

After contacting them and completing all the necessary arrangements to open the first Benetton store in each Country, we scheduled an appointment in our office to go through the collection and place the initial order of Benetton merchandise.

The day came and the appointment was at 9 am. We waited until 10 am, then 10:30, then 11 am, still no sign of the new clients.

In those years there were no cellular phones or Internet, so no way to contact them directly. I was getting nervous but suddenly our store manager came above, where the office was located, saying that a big luxury limousine was standing in front of the store, on the High Street in Reading, asking for confirmation that it was the right place.

I then went downstairs to welcome the ladies (I had never personally met them yet) and they kindly instructed the driver to wait for them until their coming back. The driver was respectfully obeying, and we went up.

When we entered the showroom, I could clearly see the astonished faces of my young staff looking at them: they saw two beautiful ladies, the Omani one was particularly beautiful, wearing high fashion very expensive clothes and incredible jewellery around their neck and hands.

It was already 11:45 when we started to look at the collection and one hour later, realizing the ladies might have been hungry, we pulled out some sandwiches we had bought that morning.

Mrs. Al Sabah said, "Oh no, please call my driver!"

The driver rushed upstairs and was instructed to bring up a "small selection of Middle Eastern food for us to enjoy."

In disbelief, we saw a full lunch for twenty people arrive upstairs, and some of it was hot! Where the hell had they been keeping it? I had no idea. So, to our embarrassment, we had lunch and then we thought we would finally start writing down the orders (in those years we had no computers yet, believe it or not!).

With our surprise, the ladies smiled and said, "The collection is wonderful, we want all the styles and all the colours you think appropriate. We fully trust your experience, so please complete the orders, and then send them to our staff, they will organize the payment." And, with that, they left.

We couldn't believe what happened: we were used to fight for the budget to be achieved, and then it was normally a very difficult exercise to create a homogeneous order since most of our clients, not professional retailers, were following their personal taste in selecting the styles, and this is the worst attitude for a buyer.

I had a funny feeling to have been dropped in the 'Benetton agent's paradise', it was like a dream!

In the meantime, we had received in our UK office a few telexes enquiring for Benetton opportunities to open stores in the Gulf area.

We then decided, with Riccardo Weiss, to go on a trip there to verify personally what this was all about and evaluate the realistic possibility of doing some business in a totally 'virgin' area, where the fashion-world best expression was 'the souk', or local open market.

I left with Riccardo from Venice to Amman, in Jordan, having obtained, a month before, all the various visas required in each Gulf country.

The first visit was in Amman, a very poor city back then. Our party there was a Jordanian that had married a young girl coming from one of the best local families and had three children with her, although we discovered, not much later, that he was gay and had an affair with his male buyer! I never understood if she knew and pretended not to, or if she was naively unaware of this situation.

He had already opened the first Benetton store in the Middle East, about 20 square metres (just bigger than a bathroom!) in the only Shopping Centre existing then. We agreed to open a second one in a new project and moved to Kuwait.

Leaving Amman on a Kuwait Airlines flight, Riccardo and I decided to have a little joke with the hostess. When, after take-off, she came around asking the passengers if they wanted a drink, I loudly asked for a "whisky on the rocks," well knowing that alcohol was strictly prohibited in Kuwait, a Muslim country.

She then told me, lowering her voice in an embarrassed murmur, "Sorry sir, in Kuwait there is no alcohol, can I give you any other drink?"

I then turned to Riccardo sitting next to me and asked, again loudly, "Rick, shall we have the usual then?"

He promptly said, "Of course!"

I then turned again to the hostess and asked, "Do you have Chanel no.5?"

She answered, "Yes sir."

I said, "Ok then, let's have two Chanel no.5 on the rocks!"

She left and we laughed between ourselves, thinking that it was obvious we were joking with her.

Instead, with our great surprise, she came back moments later with two glasses, ice, and the perfume in them! I looked at her with lack of belief and I was forced to clarify, "Sorry, we were just joking, we don't want to die drinking that stuff!" and we ordered a coke.

We then continued our trip, after Kuwait where we briefly met Mrs. Al-Sabah, only to be introduced to her staff with whom we were going to manage our business in future years.

I realized that Arabs coming from the various royal families had really nothing to do, since all their activities and needs, financial, business, and personal, were managed by either Europeans, primarily British, or Indians or Lebanese. However, it was difficult to meet them, as if they were always very busy and didn't have the time to talk to you.

Our next stop was in Dubai, where we met the two brothers, originally Iranian but born and educated in Dubai and Europe, who were not particularly wealthy or influential, but very enthusiastic and excited about Benetton, so we went along very well with them and planned some openings there as well.

The final stop was in Abu Dhabi where we met a young local from the Al-Nayan royal family, who introduced us to the early project of a new shopping mall, and we agreed to take an important location for the first Benetton store there as well.

The trip had gone incredibly well, we had planted the seeds for a growing business there, in important locations and with powerful clients and we were ready to go back to Treviso.

Waiting outside the hotel, on the departure day, for a taxi to the airport, the hotel valet raised his hand to call one from a line of waiting yellow cabs.

A car quickly drove to our position and, while the taxi driver was coming out, another yellow cab rushed in front of the first one, breaking hardly just in front of it to block it, and a furious driver came out. The two started to scream to each other in Arabic, and we understood that it was a dispute between them on the priority to collect a good client going to the airport and the relevant fee.

We just watched the scene, not knowing what to do, occasionally staring at the valet, who was coldly watching as well, doing nothing.

Soon the two started to beat each other, in a very fierce physical fight, punching and kicking!

We then called a third one, put our luggage in and left to the airport, being on our way when the other two were still wrestling on the floor.

5

New York, New York

So, at the beginning of 1984 I had a very exciting and satisfying situation, but I didn't know, then, that a sudden and unpredictable change in life was just around the corner!

One morning in January of 1984 I received a phone call from Marina Salomon, then Luciano's girlfriend, who had a natural sympathy for me and had always shown her esteem for my business attitude and working principles.

We simply had a very good and friendly relationship, and she told me, "Francesco, don't mention this to anyone, but Luciano has a situation in US where the Benetton office is run by a guy he doesn't like, and feels is not adequate for the importance of the potential market. We were discussing this the other day and he was mumbling about a possible candidate to replace the guy. I suggested your name and he was immediately quite positive about it, so I think you should expect a call from him shortly but keep it for yourself!"

I thanked Marina and didn't sleep for a couple of nights, in between the excitement of the possibility and the concern of being able to cope with such a formidable task and responsibility.

A couple of days later, Kim passed me Luciano over the phone, and he just said, "Francesco, are you somehow coming to Treviso shortly?" without making any reference to why.

I wanted to say, "I'll be there tomorrow morning!" but instead I answered, "Yes, I think I'll need to come there next week for some re-orders I have to discuss with our production team."

"Ok then," Luciano concluded, "just let Luisa know and she'll arrange an appointment with me, see you soon."

Luisa Leone was his loyal secretary, one of the best in Italy, officially recognised as such by the Italian Association.

When I met Luciano, after the usual opening pleasantries, Luciano came straight to the point. "I have a manager in our office in New York that can't cope with the task and hasn't got the strength to deal with the US market. I'm confident the USA can become one of our primary markets. We are at the beginning, and I don't want to spoil our possibilities with some wrong decisions right at the start. I need someone like you there, that I can trust and work with closely. Do you like the idea?"

I thought for a moment, as caught in surprise and not to reveal any hint of possible insider's information, and then answered, "Of course, Mr. Luciano, it would be an honour and an exciting challenge for me, of which I thank you, but on one condition."

He gave me a slightly surprised look and said, "Which one?"

"I have been," I continued, "three and a half years in UK, working very hard to build my area and a network of healthy shops, I then added the Middle East, which is now very promising after the first tests with shops in Amman, Kuwait, Dubai, and Muscat, and I don't want to lose all this for the USA. If I can keep my agent position here, I'm ready for the job."

Luciano smiled in his unique way, it was a mix of a friendly smile and the powerful icy look that reminded me of a cold-blooded killer.

"It's perfectly fine with me," he said, "just get organized with your office here in Europe, so that things will continue smoothly. I would like you to come to New York with me very soon. We must set up the division of the US market in different representative areas for the next spring/summer 1985 collection that will be ready soon and we must be fully operational by June."

The reason behind his acceptance of my request was not generosity. More simply, it had been always his philosophy that agents should be paid well, by percentage commissions on sales, so that they would have liquidity to financially, not only marketing, intervene in their area's operations.

If, for instance, as agent you had found a very good location in a mall, but your potential franchisee had pulled out from the investment at the last minute, Luciano was expecting you to take the lease, open the store and then eventually resell it to any other franchisee at later date, when possible.

Imagine that a beautiful new Mall was being completed in eight months, and you had agreed for a specific retail space there, but you had not yet defined the actual client to take the lease and open the store.

You would then, under your responsibility, place a future order of assorted goods for the store to receive for the opening season.

If you couldn't find the actual client to open, Benetton would never accept that you left that order (normally at least 4-5,000 garments all together) in their warehouse in Treviso, since it would have been a considerable loss if the goods were not eventually sold and only increased their end-of-season stock.

I have seen several times agents that had to collect the order from Benetton in Italy but did not know where to put the merchandise, since they hadn't concluded the store negotiation and lease.

It happened to me as well. One day, I was in NY and got a call from my UK office to let me know that, without any notification, a full order had been shipped to our office and invoiced to our company, not the trading one, but the actual representative. It was a disaster logistically, and a great complication for our operation.

It happened unexpectedly, given the fact that deliveries for that season where due only by the end of March of the following year, and we were in mid-December.

I then discovered that the shipment was ordered by Daniel, a guy from Argentina working in the commercial department, with whom I had a very heated exchange over the phone.

I came to know that this was a decision taken by one of the senior marketing team at Benetton.

He was an aggressive guy and had a close relationship with Luciano and he wanted to look good with him, with this manoeuvre, by creating turnover for the current year.

What happened, several times in different years, was that, if in a specific year sales didn't reach the budgeted level, and this would have been badly valued by Luciano on the performance of the sales department that this guy was heading, he would ship in advance all possible ready orders.

In this way, he was 'inflating' the present year turnover with invoices that should have been issued the following year.

I was furious. Before Christmas, I had to go back to Italy anyway, so I asked for an appointment with both men, pretending it was normal business.

I started the meeting, "I have always been responsible for my areas, I have never left uncollected or unpaid goods, either with my own shops or my clients' ones, therefore I do not tolerate that an order is shipped to my office without any advice, any prior agreement both logistically and from a payment's plan point of view. Therefore, I require that this order be collected back from my office immediately, at your expense."

It was like a bomb, neither of them (Luciano certainly knew what had happened but pretended not to) expected such an aggressive reaction, and at the end they accepted my request.

Since that episode, the marketing guy never tried to screw me again, and eventually became even a friend of mine.

As for Luciano, I knew that he liked 'men with balls' and, not being officially part of the complaint, entirely on this other colleague's shoulders, he must have liked my behaviour and, deep inside, approved it!

So, having quickly taken the necessary arrangements for the coming developments, I was ready for New York!

I arrived in Manhattan in February of 1984, with Luciano, and I was introduced to the office staff as the new executive vice-president of Benetton Services (USA) Corp., Luciano being, obviously, the president.

We were staying at the Plaza Hotel, in Central Park, and our office was at the 23rd floor of the GM Building, just opposite.

It was a small office, relatively speaking, of only 2,500 sq. ft., and we only had seven or eight employees.

The Benetton stores in USA were only 25 in total, with 10 in Manhattan itself.

My predecessor had already left, and the field was free. With Luciano, we spent the first ten days on the map of United States, discussing which representative areas to define and whom to appoint as agent.

Of course, Luciano had already in mind most of the agents, chosen between his best clients and agents in Europe, to whom he had already, in some cases, spoken and offered the position.

At the end, we came up with thirteen areas, distributed as in the following map:

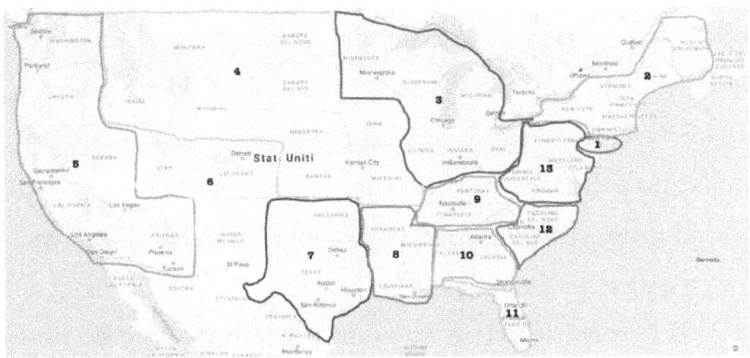

Most of the agents, as I said, were well known prime contacts of Luciano, like Paolo, Iraklis, Antonio, the Sal brothers, Antony, Walter, etc., and a few young guys that had been probably chosen because nobody really wanted to go work and live in certain areas, like Denis in Carolina, Gilberto in Louisiana, and Paolo in Alabama.

We organized the first general meeting of all agents in conjunction with the presentation of the following season collection, Autumn/Winter 1984.

In our conference room, packed with agents and their assistants, we started the usual selection. In those years, the Benetton collection had become unnecessarily huge.

In an attempt to satisfy the needs of a global market (Benetton was present in 120 countries) our design department, headed by Giuliana, the sister, had created over 1,500 different styles and, of course, we had to narrow it down to the usual 250/300 that would eventually be bought in the US market.

This exercise, by itself, was a war: everybody had his own opinion and wanted strongly some garments included or excluded, not to talk about the selection of colours, where Benetton had a general chart of over 100 colours, including prime and second shades.

But the real extraordinary event that I remember was the so called 'projection of free orders'.

This was the attempt, by each agent, to foresee how many shops he would open, in his area, through new 'franchisee' clients, for A/W 85, and it was a pure guess.

Luciano, as usual, was only interested in maximizing the sales, although 'theoretical', by getting his agents to commit to the highest orders possible, so he moved strategically in the right direction by asking first the oldest and stronger personality ones.

He knew that none of them would have wanted to look inferior to the others, or less aggressive, so he started with Armando and Paolo in California, followed by Antonio, Sal, Iraklis and so on.

The result was an insane race to the highest number of 'free orders' that ended with a total, for the USA, of over 150 orders.

This meant that, on average, each agent had to find twelve new franchisees, mall locations, and organize interior decoration (it was coming from Italy, with all relevant logistic complications of shipment's timing, duty and US regulations on electric systems, fire security and so on), its assembly and opening, all of which in six months!

I knew it was too much, but there was no way to change Luciano's approach on these things; any attempt on my side to mitigate this would have discredited me, without any practical result, so I knew I had to do my best and play with it!

We had a computer system, by then, that was directly connected to Benetton in Italy, via a dedicated line.

This meant the agents would write the orders on a paper book, send us a copy, and our staff would manually enter all the orders by terminal to Benetton; it was a huge task to complete in the fastest possible way, and my staff had to work for two weeks 24 hours round the clock!

I still remember when, after completion of the process, I received a call from my friend Riccardo Weiss, the area manager for Middle East and second in charge of marketing department, who said to me, "I don't believe this, Luciano is crazy if he accepts to put into production for next winter over 800,000 garments ordered totally blind, with no certainty they will be collected. It might result in a huge warehouse leftover that Benetton has never experienced, and, with an average cost price of $14, it means a value of $11 million! You must convince him to cut it down at least by 50%!"

"Riccardo," I said, "do you want my job here? Because if I said anything like this to Luciano, you know better than me that I would be on my way back home the following day! So, don't tell me this, we must make it happen with the lowest possible damage! We must work closely with all the agents, making sure they understand it's a critical moment and they are risking their own position right now, because if any of them leaves more than one uncollected order, which we must account for as margin of error, we'll fire that agent on the spot!"

Riccardo was silent for a few moments, then exploded. "You and Luciano are both crazy and *fatti della stessa pasta* (you are similar), it will end up that the one losing his job it's me!" He continued with unrepeatable curse words!

Besides these vital events for our future in USA (don't forget we only had twenty-five stores in total, and we were projecting to multiply by six this number in six months!), there are a few funny episodes that I recall, during that period.

First, Luciano had bought 50% of Fiorucci in 1981, the famous jeans maker in Italy, very popular already in the US as well, because he liked the creativity of Elio Fiorucci, the designer and founder of the brand. Elio was a wonderful person, gentle, smart and with a very good sense of humour, but terrible administrator. His company in Italy was on the edge of bankruptcy and the stepping in of Luciano, with some capital increase, was for Elio a manna from heaven.

Elio had Leonardo, a very capable and creative PR guy in NY, sharp in his comments that would come out in a split of a second. We were in our office, during a small party with the agents, their assistants, and few other invitees.

We had just been presented the accessories collection that were introduced, on a license agreement for the first time, by a well-established company, Hot Sox, specialized in hosiery, a Ralph Lauren's licensee as well.

The founders, who became my best friends in the following years, were Sarah and Gary Wolkowitz. They were a wonderful couple, ex-hippies from the late sixties, when in college they'd experienced the era of 'flower power'.

They started Hot Sox with very little money and made a great success of it. Sarah was also a very beautiful woman, tall and elegant, with a strong personality and sex appeal.

During the presentation of the collection, right before the Hot Sox ladies came in with the accessories, one of the agents, Paolo, left the room for the restrooms. He opened the door exactly at the same time as Sarah was coming in, and found himself face to face with her, just a few centimetres away. He froze staring at her and then, turning to all of us, asked in Venetian dialect, "Chi zea sta gran figa?" (Who is this beautiful woman?). The translation doesn't really match the Italian-Venetian meaning. *Figa* is the Italian slang word for 'vagina', literally, but it really means 'a beautiful sexy woman you would gladly have sex with on the spot'!

We exploded laughing and Sarah, of course, couldn't understand why.

In the following years, when we were good friends and had a total familiarity, I then explained the real meaning to her, for which she too was laughing, as well as little pleased for the dashing compliment.

Leonardo, at the end, was asking Paolo if he were always that much attracted by beautiful women, and he naively answered, "Of course, yes, if you come and see me in Nashville, I will introduce you to some beautiful sexy ladies!"

We all laughed loudly, as he was proud of his macho attitude, without realizing we were instead laughing about his stupidity, given the fact that Leonardo was gay, and Paolo had been the only one not to understand it!

During those days, we went for dinner with all the agents and Luciano at Gallagher Steak House.

We were a big table for twenty people, and at the end, when I asked for the check that I would usually pay with my credit card of 'Benetton USA', strangely Luciano told me, "I will pay the check tonight."

So, I gave his credit card to the waiter, thinking, *He probably wants everybody to see that he is offering the dinner, for some reason.*

He signed the debit slip (in those days it had to be manually printed in carbon copy with the card visible!) and we left.

The agents were already outside; it was snowing, windy, a terribly cold night. As a gesture of respect, they had already stopped the first yellow cab and offered it to me and Luciano. I opened the door of the cab when suddenly Luciano told me, lowering his voice, "We have to go back in, I made a mistake with the credit card."

So, we did and, when in, he continued "I gave them my personal credit card instead of the Italian corporate one of Benetton Group."

We then had to go through the entire procedure of voiding the previous transaction with a refund form and issue a new one. All this, manually, took another 20 minutes.

The only explanation I could find was that Luciano wasn't sure that his personal receipt would have been tax-deductible in Italy and refunded to him by the company, and therefore he decided to redo it, otherwise he would have personally paid the ¾ of the check pertaining to his three siblings. It made me laugh that a multimillionaire guy was so frustrated at the idea of losing, in favour of his siblings, some $800!

In July 1985, Luciano Benetton told me a very interesting story about banks.

We were walking from our head-office in 59 street and Madison in Manhattan, to the nearby office of Citibank.

I was walking with Luciano, ahead of another group, which included Gilberto Benetton, our managing director Aldo Palmeri (the best ever at Benetton!), and few others.

We were going to sign the first syndicated loan to Benetton S.p.A. for $30,000,000, arranged by Citibank, with funds provided by several other banks such as Bank of America, The Bank of New York, Chemical Bank, The First National Bank of Boston, etc.

Aldo Palmeri had explained to me that we did not really need this money, which would be used to replace some medium-term debt in Italy, but it was 'politically' important because it was introducing us to the American financial establishment, in view of our imminent flotation on the stock exchange in Milan.

Luciano, walking besides me, said, "It is funny that now all these banks are begging us to accept their credit lines. When I started in the sixties, I needed Lit. 500,000, the equivalent of $4,000 in present value, and they asked me all sorts of guarantees. I had to beg a friend of mine to come and sign for me; otherwise, I wouldn't get the money.

Now they are begging us to accept $ 30 million and they would give us more if we asked. If they only knew that I felt much more confident about my future then, rather than now…"

He meant that he had a clear view of the market opportunities in his early days, and felt absolutely sure about his future success, while now the competition was fierce and our future much less predictable. He confirmed, with my great pleasure, my feelings about banks.

As a friend of mine put it, "Banks would give you the umbrella when it stops raining."

The flotation in Milan was a big success, mainly because the family put only 30% of the share in public offer. With this small percentage (contrary to the concept of "Public Company") they wanted to retain full control of the operation and a board that wouldn't be too… invasive!

At that time Benetton was offering some preferential shares to their management and I remember receiving a call from one of our Finance internal mangers telling me:

"You'll receive a call from BSI, the Swiss bank in Lugano, to propose to you the finance of the shares purchase in advance." Being very busy at that time with all that was going on with Benetton USA, I wasn't really concentrated on this issue, so I took this call and when I was asked how much would I like to invest (on the basis that BSI would finance me without any 'guarantee' to provide, and this sounded very strange, it was the first time I was offered a line of credit without having to come up with some sort of collateral!) I answered, "A billion lire," (the equivalent of half a million Euros).

It's one of my regrets, since selling those shares a few months later gave me a profit of 85% on the investment, probably the easiest money I've ever had in the short term! Had I paid more attention, I could have bought much more than that and therefore generate a much bigger profit…!

In the same period, July 1985, the largest live concert ever on the planet took place: Live Aid.

It was a huge event, and we had been invited to participate, somehow, as Benetton in USA.

We did so and sold a particular sweatshirt, a kind of 'rugby shirt', on which a substantial percentage of the sales went in charity to Live Aid.

6

The Manhattan War

Luciano left back to Italy, and I started my activity in all the US, keeping in touch with all the representative offices and monitoring the progression of orders.

I immediately realized that most agents felt of having a privileged relationship with Luciano, and therefore they were ready to follow their own path, disregarding the guidelines coming from the Benetton USA's office. I had to use an iron fist right from the beginning or else I would have lost my authority.

The occasion came immediately in Manhattan itself.

Nara was a major client in Milan and had gone into partnership with the Sal and John brothers and Benetton itself since the beginning, opening the early Benetton stores.

Luciano, who had been always a convinced supporter of the concept that 'competition is healthy', let others come into the Manhattan market. A company was owned by Hermann, a Jewish originally from Germany, who was in partnership with another big Italian client in Italy, Nilo, and finally the Wallis from London, once big retailers there, now somehow less powerful and financially rumoured, that were only interested in big locations and searching a good one for a 'megastore'.

Hermann called me and said, "Sal has more shops than us, they've been taking the best locations, we would be happy to at least open a store in a residential area, not a great location, but we feel it could be doing well because it's on 93rd St and Madison, a rich area in the Upper East side."

I went with him to look at the location and, after discussing the possible rent and other things, I finally gave him the OK to go ahead and, of course, I notified the other clients of the future opening.

After a few days I got a call from a real estate broker who said to me that, "It's pretty stupid that the bidding for the available location on 93rd Street, pushing up the rent almost every other day, is coming not from a different brand, but two Benetton operators."

I couldn't believe what I was hearing and asked who the second bidder was. He asked me not to mention him, because he also had some business in the past with them, and confirmed it was Sal.

Now, here we were: two Benetton clients were hurting our performance by both bidding on the same location, a suicidal strategy.

That was not acceptable! I called John and asked him to immediately withdraw any offer, as Hermann had already been given the green light. He accepted but it was clear that he wasn't happy.

A couple of days later I was informed that Sal was still in the picture, so I called back John and asked him, very angrily, what was going on and why he didn't withdraw. He answered what I had already figured out that "Walter has spoken to Luciano and Luciano told him he could go ahead."

Either I could stop this, or I was ready to be executed on the battlefield of Benetton in USA.

I called immediately Luciano and referred what I had been told and asked him if that was true. He said, "Walter called me and said that Hermann was too greedy and would have lost the location; there were other brands interested and it was necessary to offer the proper rent immediately or else we would lose the store for good. So, I told him to go ahead."

I answered "Mr. Luciano, all the people involved here in the USA have a direct line with you from years, and the result is they will never respect me as the director of operations in USA, thinking they can talk to you directly. Sal and Walter are clearly trying to get rid of Hermann as a competitor. This is playing dirty and is negative for all of us and our reputation in the Real Estate market, where we look like idiots! Either you fully trust me and save my authority, or it's better I stop straight away. I'm therefore asking you to call Nara explaining the situation and confirming they will never open that store, even if they sign a lease, or you have my resignation with immediate effect."

I remember very well that Luciano was silent for a few seconds, then said, "I didn't expect them to do this. I understand, you are right, I will call Walter and tell him to let it go."

That was a crucial moment in my career with Benetton, it was when Luciano thought, *This guy has balls!* And such interference never happened again.

As a matter of fact, Walter decided to withdraw from Manhattan at the end of 1985 and, when Luciano came back to US on one of his trips, he said to me, "Francesco, as you know, our policy is to be in partnership with someone in the beginning if that helps to acquire a good location or to open a new market, but I believe we are an industry, not a retailer, and ultimately it's better if we stay out of it. Walter is also getting older and said he would like to withdraw from Manhattan, so we decided that Sal could acquire some of the stores owned by B&A Apparel, our company, and then we could sell the shares of B&A to you."

I looked at him with probably a sceptical face.

He continued with a smile, "Of course, I understand this is, even at cost, quite a financial commitment, so I will give you the agency for Manhattan itself. Form your own representative company, in another separate office, and you will take care of the agency as well."

I smiled back, didn't question this, and said yes.

Now, from the financial point of view, Manhattan turnover at industrial cost was at that time around $16 million and with an agent commission of 6.25% (it was higher than the 5% used in Italy because of higher running costs), I had a million a year to allow me to run my separate office, not too bad!

I then created my own corporation which was operating the representative office of Benetton for the city of New York, where the total shops owned by independent licensees by 1987 became 31 and total sales were in the region of $ 35 million.

I was going back and forward from UK to USA regularly and still being based at The Plaza, with my wife and my daughter Simona living in the UK.

I had already been a couple of months in Manhattan, and, among others, I had met one of the attorneys working with Benetton, Bruce, a very nice person.

With him, I had signed all the paperwork related to my new position and he gave me all the necessary information on various aspects of living in New York, either legal, commercial, or personal. Being the executive vice-president, he asked me what my yearly remuneration and benefits were. I had agreed nothing.

He was shocked, but he couldn't understand the different basis of my relationship with Benetton and the Italian way of thinking.

He said, "Well, you'll have to tell us what to set you for, we have to obtain for you a social security number and we need a full contract with your employer, Benetton USA, with all the details!"

"Ok Bruce," I said, "when I come back the next time, I'll have everything fixed for you."

I went to Italy for various matters, and met with Gilberto to discuss these details, Luciano would never talk about these matters, he always referred to Gilberto.

I said, "Mr. Gilberto, after two months in NY, now that we know I'm going to be there for good, we need to arrange an employment contract necessary for my visa, social security, etc.

How do you want me to arrange this?"

Now, in a normal world, your boss would have offered some terms, non-negotiable, but in line with the market.

Gilberto, instead, said, "You tell me Francesco, how much do you want?" I was expecting this, it was a trap.

Had I asked too much, I would have irritated the Benetton, too little would have looked silly, so I said, "Manhattan is a very expensive city, and so some benefits are a must: accommodation and school for my daughter (my family was going to join me later in 1985 in NYC).

"I have found an apartment on 95th and Madison and the monthly Rent is $5,000 and the school is quarterly $10,000." I could see in his eyes that he was thinking "Expensive, in Italy it wouldn't be possible!" but he couldn't object.

And then he said, "How about your remuneration?" this was the sensitive issue. Bear in mind I was already an agent for UK and Middle East, so I was making a very nice profit at the end of the year, I couldn't show to be greedy, not for their mentality.

"Well," I continued, "a normal salary for my position would be around $250,000 net, but I would be happy with $40,000."

Gilberto was satisfied and we discussed the last small details of my contract.

That was a period of intense activity, with Luciano coming to New York basically 10 days almost every month.

I was working closely with him on a daily basis, and it was not difficult once you understood the guy.

As I said before, he was an apparently very calm person, even gentle in his manners and never arrogant with people around him.

I often thought that any other person would have been much worse in his position: after all, at that precise moment, he was one of the most famous people in the world, his brand was considered one of the top five worldwide and almost all newspapers and magazines had dedicated an article or interview to him.

So, his simplicity and behaviour were the sign of a very intelligent and sensitive person, in fact Luciano was the best listener I ever encountered.

Any other in his shoes would have taken the centre stage and would have talked and talked and made sure that everybody around knew how much intelligent and capable he was!

Luciano was instead mainly listening to others, 'perceiving' their personalities and qualities, good and bad, and very quickly determining which strategy to use with them, for his own benefit.

In this sense, I have considered him almost a 'genius'.

I say almost, because I think 'genius' is a term we wrongly use, in our modern society, for anybody with success in his business or sector, and I strongly believe it's wrong.

If we search the definition of 'genius', we find:

'Extraordinary intellectual power especially as manifested in creative activity, a person endowed with extraordinary mental superiority.'

I agree with this and then, a genius is Leonardo da Vinci, or Aristotle, or Stephen Hawking and so on, not Luciano or any other successful person that, at most, can be considered 'very intelligent'.

He was really capable of keeping his composure, staying very calm even in the face of emergencies or sudden developments of events. In 30 years working with him, I have seen him lose his temper only twice.

The first time it was in his office in Ponzano, when he got a call during one of our personal meetings, and he suddenly became infuriated and said something like, "I would open his body and take his guts out on the floor!"

I was almost shocked to hear such a strong statement and I still don't know, to this date, who was the subject of his fury, but it was definitely related to someone in business who had done something very wrong with him.

The second time was in New York, it was a freezing day in January, and we were walking to Harry's Bar for some lunch, and he had received a call from London just a moment before leaving the office.

He was strangely serious and mumbling something, until he exploded saying to me, "If he were here, I would kick him in his balls from here to Harry's Bar!"

Surprised by this aggressiveness, I asked him who was he talking about, and he answered me, looking straight ahead, "My son Rocco, he is always creating some trouble!"

I knew Rocco; he was fifteen at that time, an exuberant kid that had been sent to London to stay and work there to take him out of his ambience in Treviso, where he had some wrong friends.

I fully understood why his father was saying that.

7

The Real Flavio Briatore

I met Flavio when I arrived in NY, back in 1984.

He was then living in St. Thomas, US Virgin Islands, since he had left Italy overnight to avoid being arrested in a famous scandal of *bische clandestine* (private illegal gambling rooms), where some rich industrialists of the Milan area had lost fortunes. A famous TV presenter, Emilio Fede, friend of Flavio and supposedly an accomplice of the scam, had been also involved. Through Fede he had met Luciano and became his friend, although Luciano had never been gambling, he just liked to play occasionally scopa, a local Venetian game, for no money.

Flavio had been warned by some whistleblower in the police and left with just his passport to St. Thomas, where he had a house on the beach.

From there he had to move very carefully since there was an Interpol warrant, and he would be coming into US only when Luciano arrived, for a few days.

His problem with this investigation went on for some time, but it eventually concluded with an amnesty in 1990 and he was free to go back to his normal life.

In 1984 he was married to a young, blond American model who told my ex-wife that she wanted to have a baby. When I heard this from her, at the first opportunity alone with Flavio I said, "So, you'll be a father soon!"

He stared at me and said, "What?"

"Well, your wife confessed last night that you are planning to have a baby."

"Look," he said, "the only son I could have would be an eighteen-year-old boy, with a personal net worth of $100 million, to adopt!"

We both exploded with laughter! A few months later, he divorced.

Flavio was brilliant, pleasant but not exactly the most trustworthy person on hearth. He had opened, during his exile in Virgin Islands, three Benetton stores and they were doing very well, so he kept busy and at the same time he was making enough money to live the way he always lived before, in luxury!

However, I started having some problems, since the administrative office of Benetton in Italy was calling me because of some unpaid invoices of his company and, knowing he was a friend of Luciano, they didn't know what to do. I didn't either.

When Luciano came back to NY the next time, I asked him what I had to do with Flavio, and he said candidly, "Make him pay our invoices, of course! You see, I like Flavio, he is a nice guy and an intelligent person, but I would never give him my wallet! As a matter of fact, a couple of years ago we were five friends at Flavio's home in St Thomas for a short holiday: me, Marina (his girlfriend at the time), Ugo (he was the agent in Milan, one of the most influential in Italy, since the Lombardia region was generating a turnover for Benetton of 180 billion Italian lire, or 10% of its total turnover!) and Walter.

"Flavio wanted to start with the first store in St Thomas and asked us to enter in partnership because he didn't have all the necessary capital here in US, as in Italy his accounts were blocked. So, we put $10,000 each and with $50,000 he opened the store. The store was doing well and the next time I saw Flavio I told him that I had done this just to help him out and that I would rather not be involved with the company in Virgin Island and asked him to buy me out. So, Flavio gave me back the $10k while the other three associates still didn't know that I was out!"

Luciano told me this with a big smile, liking the idea that he had outsmarted his girlfriend and the other two associates and now he would be sitting comfortably watching what would happen! He was like this; these little games really amused him!

A couple of years later Ugo called me from Milan and asked me, on behalf of Marina as well, if I could help them getting back their $10k each because they had tried several times with Flavio, with no success. I didn't get involved.

Going back to the unpaid invoices, I used to call Flavio over the phone (we had developed in the meantime a friendly relationship) and asked him about the outstanding payments and he would say, "Oh, I just mailed the checks to you the other day!"

Inevitably, the checks never arrived, and I had occasionally to take a plane, go there to spend a nice weekend and with that, sit down with him and force him to give me post-dated checks to plan the payments for the following months.

During one of these trips, we went out with his speedboat, a nice 'cigarette', very fast, and a few friends including some beautiful girls. Flavio always liked beautiful girls and he knew how to handle them!

The day was cloudy, and I was without a T-shirt when Flavio told me, "Put some protection on, although clouded the sunlight here is very powerful."

I minimized the matter, ignoring the advice for skin protection, which was a very silly decision on my part! When I got back, I was as red as a pack of Marlboros, and shaking with a high temperature in my bedroom.

A big black lady came in, sent by Flavio, who smiled at me and said, "You poor white guy, you want to do the same things we black people do and look at yourself!"

I felt like a total idiot.

"Don't worry, I'll take care of you," she said, then left.

She was back a few minutes later with a machete in her right hand and a big 'aloe' leaf in her left one. She sliced the leaf in its long side and collected all the gel from it, then putting it all over my body (I was naked, shaking on the bed, feeling I would die!), then repeating the application until she sliced the entire leaf, and I was covered all over with the gel.

"Now," she told me, "sleep well and I'll come and call you for dinner!"

I thought she was kidding me, I would never be able to have dinner, I felt sick; nevertheless, I fell asleep immediately.

At 8 pm, a couple of hours later, she came, woke me up and I went for a shower: miraculously my skin had lost most of the redness and I felt much better!

I thanked her and kissed her, telling her she saved my life, and gave her a good tip! She was giggling and thanking me and wished me a happy dinner with Flavio and our friends.

In 1989 I brought to Manhattan the famous Italian restaurant Paper Moon. It was an icon in Milan, where all the buyers and fashion designers were going for lunch and dinner, always full and with a beautiful crowd of models, actors, and VIPs.

The owner was a simple guy that had the brilliant idea of combining the freshness of a pizzeria with the good food of a restaurant and he did so some years earlier, in 1977, in Via Bagutta, a parallel of Via Montenapoleone. When this became the heart of the high fashion in Milan and in the world, he found himself in the perfect spot to be successful. I met Pio like anybody else, in his restaurant, and we became friends.

When I went to NY, I found out that his model had already been copied by an Italian guy that opened in uptown 3rd Avenue, with the name 'Mezzaluna'. It was an immediate success, with the typical Italian flair: all the waiters were nice looking young boys, with a white shirt and black pants and apron, and a (fake) Rolex on their wrist. They were always smiling, cracking jokes, and welcoming any lady coming in with a "Ciao bella!" (It means "Hi beautiful!") and, as a result, all the female clients were in love with them and the male ones were going there, both for the ladies and to enviously study the behaviour of the waiters.

I convinced Pio that his 'original' operation, with a name already famous internationally among the fashion crowd, would have made a lot of money in Manhattan, but it would need a prime location. I became a partner in it and would guarantee all the local organization for him impossible (he didn't speak any English), and he would provide the know-how and management of the new restaurant.

We found an almost perfect spot on 59th St. between Madison and Park Ave, a large 6,000 sq. ft. place that was projected and decorated by Pio's Italian architect Dal Lago. It was an important investment for us of over a million dollars, at that time, but it went very well, averaging 500 clients a day mostly at lunch, and a turnover of over $6 million in the first year. We eventually sold it shortly afterwards for a very nice profit.

Our restaurant was exactly above a new discotheque-lounge that became the number one in Manhattan that year, when the well-known Howard Stein opened "Au Bar" in 1988.

We quickly developed a synergy with Au Bar, sending our good clients to each other and in those days a significant episode took place with Flavio Briatore. He was in town for a couple of weeks from Saint Thomas, US Virgin Islands, and we saw each other every day, for lunch or dinner. That night I had arranged a dinner with an English Interior Decorator, a nice young lady, who told me that she was with a couple of friends she was working with on their project of a new luxury apartment in NY, and when I asked whether I knew any of them, she naively said, "I don't know, one is Reza." I asked, "Reza who?" (Thinking, "Could he be the one?) and she followed with "Reza Pahlavi, the son of the Shah of course!"

Later that day, Flavio called me and asked, "Where are you dining tonight?"

"Here at Paper Moon," I answered, "we're having dinner with some friends from London."

He continued with an annoyed voice, "Anybody I know?"

I said, "I don't think so, maybe Reza?"

"Reza who?"

"Reza Pahlavi." Then, he suddenly arrived first, immediately attracted by the pompous name of the son of the Shah!

This was Flavio, a nice, simpatico, and exuberant guy only interested in success, money, and connections. He booked the best table for us all at Au Bar, where after dinner he treated Reza with Dom Perignon and a bunch of beautiful girls he knew, shortly becoming best friend with him!

In Europe he had been a good friend of Philippe Junot, the ex-husband of Princess Caroline of Monaco, and they were both going to the Jimmy'z Monte Carlo, opened in the 70s by the great Regine, good friend of Philippe.

Flavio liked that place very much and, when he was confined in Saint Thomas, he thought of opening one there, for all the tourists arriving on the beautiful island. However, he didn't have the money to do it and even if he did, he wouldn't want to use his own money, a good habit he carried with him all his life.

He finally met a guy from Puerto Rico who was manufacturing shirts and overalls for the US army. Flavio introduced him to me in NY during one of his trips and asked me a favour. "I'm working on this guy to finance a disco I want to open in St Thomas exactly like the Regine's one "Jimmy'z" in Monte Carlo, it's a phenomenal success! He wants to manufacture shirts for the Benetton brand in Puerto Rico and, even if you are not interested, please pay him a visit there just to keep him happy, showing some possibility of arranging that, you understand? I need some time to make him pull the money!" "Ok Flavio" I said, "I'll go there with my CFO for a day or two and play the game."

Sometime later, we went to his factory, a large facility with 2,000 ladies working on manufacturing these items in a big production line. We were talking about all this from his office located in the mezzanine level, with a big window looking down to the working place, from where he could control his operation.

At a certain point he said to me "Let's go down, I want to show you the very precise details of the stitching we are obliged by the US Army," and he gave me a kind of gas mask, saying, "We better wear this, there is carbon powder in the layer inside the military combat overall, quite toxic."

While going down, I noticed none of the ladies was using one. When we went back to the office, and we took off the mask, I asked him, "Why don't you provide a mask to your workers?"

He said, quite nervously, "Well they don't deal with this material every day and they are… used to it, anyway… don't worry!"

I suddenly stood up and said, very angrily, "I do worry! And you should as well for the life of 2,000 poor local ladies desperately in need of the shitty salary you pay them! I'll make sure that, as long as I am the president on Benetton USA, you'll never work with us!" and I left the room and Puerto Rico.

Afterwards Flavio called me and asked "What the f... happened there? I asked you to keep him happy, not to insult him!"

"Flavio," I said, "your friend is a dirty guy, a kind of man I strongly despise, and I don't want to see him again. You can do what you want with him but keep him out of my office!"

He then calmed down and said, "Well, fortunately, he has already agreed to do Jimmy'z and to finance it all!"

He eventually opened Jimmy'z a year later, were we had some very exciting nights, the place was nice and went well, but I learnt later of two problems: the first that Regine was infuriated because Flavio had no permission to use the name and didn't pay any royalty to her, and the second that Jimmy'z went up in flames shortly afterwards with a big fight for the insurance to be collected.

8

Flavio, Alessandro Benetton, Michael Schumacher and F1

There have been many stories about the adventure of Benetton in Formula 1 and its manager, Flavio Briatore, but none of them explains what really happened.

Benetton had been a sponsor in F1 for many years, since 1983 when they started with the British team Tyrrell. They then continued with the Alfa Romeo team and Riccardo Patrese, who was a very fast driver, although particularly aggressive with the mechanic parts: his engineer told me in the box that when they dismantled the car after a race, as they always do, the clutch and gear were to throw away, destroyed!

Luciano was tired of spending quite some money (a few million dollars) in a sponsorship that didn't generate any return of money or, at least, image. The teams were in the bottom part of the standings with very little visibility.

He then decided to ask our PR director and famous journalist and presenter, Davide Paolini, to re-think the advertising / sponsorship strategy for the future, maybe abandoning F1. Paolini started analysing the structure of F1 and came up with a very smart and logical conclusion: only the actual teams were visible, the Sponsors being only visible and talked about in TV or photos published immediately after a race. Nobody was talking, in a bar or street, of Marlboro, Camel, Benetton, etc. but of Ferrari, Mc Laren, Williams and so on. Shortly, everybody's attention was for the racing teams, their pilots, and the wild competition to get the Championship at the end of the year.

In 1985 the British team Toleman was on the edge of bankruptcy having lost their contract with Michelin and therefore being literally without tires to race with.

Paolini had a brilliant idea and met with Luciano and Gilberto and said, "We have a unique opportunity, we can buy a F1 team, well organized and efficient, for a very small amount and call it "Benetton Formula" and compete under our own brand name. In this way all TV's, Sport Magazines and newspapers will talk about us! Not only, we then find sponsors, like us today, that will pay for advertising on our cars, and our minimum target will be to break even at the end of the year, instead of spending millions like today.

What we need is just a different approach, bringing our colourful vision to the stiff and old- fashioned world of F1: let's make our cars very colourful, like our sweaters, and everybody will talk about them!"

They did so, to the point of colouring the tires in yellow, green, and red and it was a smash!

The team went on with moderate performances, until Luciano thought, in 1989, that it needed someone more dynamic and with an entrepreneurial view, rather than a technical manager, as they had so far. His son Alessandro had already become president, but it needed the support of a more experienced and sharper general manager.

Luciano thought Flavio could be the right person. He asked him if he were interested, and Flavio immediately took the challenge on.

There are some very important events that are crucial and unknown to this date.

When Flavio arrived at F1, of course he knew very little of racing cars and was however very lucky to find a person that would become his best adviser, behind the scenes: Tom Walkinshaw. The ex-pilot knew very well the world of racing and was the mind behind all the best technical decisions made in those years, like the arrival of Ross Brawn in 1991 to replace John Barnard and the return, very important, of Rory Byrne. Together they created the winning car for Schumacher.

But let's go back for a moment to the arrival of Flavio: Luciano, as usual, didn't get involved with any financial decision and therefore said to Flavio "Go and talk to Gilberto for your contract." Gilberto was what in US would be called the CFO of the company and was employed in a bank when Luciano, after starting his manufacturing with his sister Giuliana, convinced him to join them in the new venture.

Gilberto didn't have a sophisticated background and no university degree, but was very practical and very good in evaluating people around him and choosing the best collaborators, such as Gianni Mion who became his 'right-hand man' for most of his life, or Aldo Palmeri, the MD that arrived from Banca d'Italia in 1984 and was the one to convince the siblings to go public in 1985 and made Benetton an international corporation.

(When, by the way, just floating 30% of the company on the Milan stock exchange, the family made about €150 million that allowed them to start other acquisitions in other sectors, with Gilberto at the head of Edizione Holding, the family 'safe').

So, Flavio met with Gilberto who wasn't sure which kind of financial compensation to discuss with him, not being familiar with F1 positions and asked Flavio to make a request, thinking that from there he would negotiate down.

With his surprise, Flavio asked a very reasonable fixed salary and a scheme of 'bonus' based on improvement of performance of Benetton Formula: the previous year, 1988, Benetton was third in the Constructors' F1 Championship with 39 points, and it was almost impossible to foresee an improvement on that, with the car and pilots (Nannini and Boutsen) they had.

So Flavio shot high and said, "You'll pay me only for points in excess of this year result but, since it will be very difficult for me to even make an extra point, you'll give me $100 thousand dollars for each extra point I'll generate."

Gilberto thought that he didn't risk anything, since an extra point in F1 classification meant much more financially from the F1 organization guided by Bernie Ecclestone, and so he agreed.

As a result, the team made 71 points in 1990, which meant a nice $3.2 million for Flavio, with Gilberto biting his fingers for having been too generous!

In 1991 Tom told Flavio that there was a new young German driver who, in his opinion, had an extraordinary potential, and who had already done some driving tests with Jordan: Michael Schumacher.

Tom said to Flavio, "However, I think it will be very difficult to grab him. Jordan, I heard from a whistleblower, has already prepared a contract for him." And this is when Flavio proved to be the manager that could make the difference: anybody else would have tried to negotiate with Jordan, Flavio instead decided to move fast and beat his rival and decided to immediately leave for Germany to meet Schumacher.

Benetton Formula's lawyer was David Mills (I met him in 1981 and we were friends by then) and I was in his office one day to discuss some legal matter involving 'franchising agreements' in the UK (a weak point for Benetton, which was sued at various times because of this), when David received a phone call and I heard him say, "Flavio, I cannot do it, I have a very important legal matter tomorrow morning in court where I absolutely need to be present".

Then he was silent for a while, then said, "Come on, Flavio, you don't need to be like this…" He was silent again, his face getting white and his look between angry and concerned, and then "Ok, ok! I'll be there!" and hung up.

I said, "Was it Briatore, David?"

He said, "Yes, he wants me to be at Heathrow in 45 minutes to go with him and Walkinshaw to Germany, for a very important matter, apparently. And he threatened me to lose Benetton altogether as a client if I don't go!" After a pause, he said, "I guess I'll have to go, excuse me, we'll continue whenever you want upon my return, just let me know when."

"Don't worry, David!" I said, "I know Flavio and it's his typical behaviour, but you'll find out that there must be something important in this sudden request, he doesn't waste time for nothing!"

And so, the three of them went to the native Schumacher's town, Hurth. They stayed in a small hotel for three days, and would have stayed longer, if necessary, until they had eventually convinced Michael and his parents to sign a contract with Benetton Formula.

We must remember that Michael's parents were of humble origin, his father was a construction worker, and at the end a contract for five years for the twenty-two-year-old pilot had to be considered a great opportunity, particularly from a financial point of view: Michael was signed for

$250k a year, a huge amount for him at that time, when he was making very little in the world of racing.

So, they left Germany very satisfied, with Schumacher in their bag. They would later compensate Jordan by giving them for free the pilot had been chosen for the year: Moreno.

As we all know, Schumacher and the team became very successful and won the first title in 1994, but by the end of the year Renault declared that it wouldn't supply engines any more to independent teams, and so the Benetton team was in trouble.

Here Flavio started his masterpiece: knowing that Ligier had a contract for the following year's supply of Renault engines, and that it was in bad financial terms, he went to Luciano and Gilberto and said, "We can buy the Ligier team for a reasonable price and then transfer the Renault engines to our team."

The Benettons were excited by the idea, but there was a problem. Gilberto said, "Fine Flavio, it could be done, but we are already rumoured in the financial circle of Milan because we have bought a team and the question would be why we would spend a lot of money in another team, particularly being a public company. We can't afford this, so I suggest we finance you and you personally buy Ligier."

Flavio immediately said, "It's fine for me, let me negotiate the purchase so that we know the amount to finance and then we'll move ahead."

Flavio bought Ligier for approximately $15 million, and that was financed by Benetton Holding in Luxembourg with an official return contract spread over ten years at low interest.

It was a very good year and Schumacher won the title by only one point ahead of Damon Hill. Benetton continued winning in 1995, both titles, and subsequently Schumacher went to Ferrari and put, as primary condition, that Ross Brawn and Rory Byrne went as well to Ferrari. This tells you how strong the chemistry between the three men was.

By the end on 1995 Peugeot, pressed by some French politicians, wanted to create an 'all French' team.

Peugeot then, like the Benettons did, sent Alain Prost as 'front man' to negotiate the purchase of Ligier and he agreed with Briatore an unofficial price of $100 million.

At this point Flavio went to the Benetton brothers and said, "I have sold the Ligier team and want to close the finance with your holding, so give me the amount of capital and interest still outstanding and I will settle it immediately."

The Benettons were stunned, and Gilberto said, "But Flavio… we had financed you not to appear as the buyers of Ligier, but we did it for our F1 team and if now Ligier is sold, it should be our money!"

Flavio maintained his cool attitude and insisted on his interpretation that it was merely a financial agreement and that he was the beneficiary of the ownership and therefore of the sale proceeds.

Legally, they couldn't oppose this reality, since in full trust they hadn't signed anything to this extent and had to swallow the manoeuvre with which Flavio made the first step towards the 'billionaire' status he was seeking!

Luciano was very disturbed by this and didn't speak to Flavio for a few years and they finally reconciled only when Flavio asked him to be his best man at his wedding with Gregoraci.

Another interesting anecdote during those years came from Alessandro Benetton.

In 1994, the year of the first F1 title of Schumacher, he came to Dubai, where I was living, to officialise a joint venture with a company I had established in the free zone of Jebel Ali.

I had obtained from Luciano the license to manufacture shoes and accessories with the "United Colors of Benetton" label for the Middle East and I was of course outsourcing the products in far-east and elsewhere, and we were growing rapidly.

Alessandro had by then established, with the financial help of his uncle Gilberto and the family, a financial company called 21 Investimenti that was acquiring shares in small companies that seemed interesting and with a growth potential that would justify the stepping in of 21 as a partner.

One of these was Enervit, an Italian company in Milan, which Alessandro wanted to promote in the Middle East, and we agreed terms for a joint venture that he came to sign for at Easter 1994.

The F1 championship had started, and Schumacher had won the first two races and was leading the F1 championship.

We were out for dinner in a nice Iranian restaurant in Deira, the old part of Dubai located on the other side of the 'creek', and I said, "Well, Alessandro, you must be very happy about the performance of the team and particularly of Schumacher, this could be a fantastic year if it continues like this!"

He smiled and said, "Yes, we are very positive and confident we have the best technical bunch of people in F1 at this time and Flavio is doing a great job!" then he became more serious and continued. "But don't think Michael is an easy guy to manage."

"I guess a champion has a different approach and must be asking almost perfection not only from himself, but from the rest of the people around him!" I commented, and told him about a situation in our Benetton Formula headquarters in Oxford, UK, when I brought in some top managers from Barclays Bank to see the facility. Our guide through the various departments was Ross Brawn, who said, "If the same car was given to all the F1 drivers, Schumacher would be at least half a second a lap faster than anybody else!" He really believed Michael was a phenomenal driver.

Alessandro went on, "Yes, that's true, but Michael has been a disappointment for me because I discovered he is very much money-oriented. You know what happened a few months ago, before the end of the year?"

"No, what happened?"

He said, "He asked for a personal meeting with me and when we met, after the usual exchange of formalities, he suddenly asked me if I knew how much Berger was making at Ferrari. I said I didn't, and he explained that Berger, who had only 12 points the previous year in 8th position, while he had 52 in 4th position, was getting $3.5 million from Ferrari, and he was only making $250k in our team and this could not be acceptable, he wanted an adequate increase in his contract."

He went on, "I explained to Michael that contracts are meant to be a serious obligation for both parties, that's why they are made so articulated and complex, and so the contract he signed with us for five years, with still three years to go, and was for him a fantastic opportunity to drive in F1 at his very young age, should have been respected as a commitment for both of us. But he was stubborn in emphasizing that he was worth much more than Berger, and on that I could agree, and therefore he had to be paid more.

"We continued to argue on the subject for almost an hour, when suddenly Michael, standing up ready to leave the room, said to me: 'Well, Alessandro, if you are not prepared to review my contract for next year, perhaps I won't be quite so motivated.' Then he left the room without saying another word. I'm sure he was joking, but still…"

I commented, "This is unbelievable, what did you do?"

"Well," he answered. "After consulting with Flavio, we had no other choice than pleasing him and upgrade his salary!"

He didn't tell me how much Michael was making at the end for the following year, but it must have been a substantial increase, close or even higher than the Berger's one!

9

Benetton and the Best Years in USA, with NBC, Outlet Stores, David Stern and NBA, Elio Fiorucci and Arrigo Cipriani

Our expansion was going extremely well, we had become very popular in USA to the extent that they gave us the nickname of 'Green Mushrooms', because we were popping up everywhere!

When I arrived in Manhattan, in 1984, we had more or less 25 stores in USA, mainly New York and LA.

By the end on 1987, three years later, we had in excess of 750 stores all over USA, after a growth of average 120 stores per season, or 240 stores a year, with retails sales of $250 million!

A phenomenon that caught the interest of NBC as well.

One day Sally, our PR, came into my office very agitated and said, "You won't believe who contacted me today!" with a big smile.

"Who?" I asked

After enjoying the moment for a few seconds, she said, "NBC producers!"

I was surprised too and asked her the details. Apparently, the TV network had decided to run a special on this newcomer from Italy in the fashion business, trying to bring to the public attention the secrets behind such a great success.

So, we started to meet with them and discuss the possibility of such special that was going to be shown during the Today Show, with a huge audience across the country.

The NBC head producer for the show was an intelligent, very active woman who started to work very closely on the project with me, and I soon realized that she had developed a kind of attraction for me.

One day we were in my office, and she had given me a script that she wanted me to read and would have gone in the broadcast because, she said, "I have never heard such a sexy male voice as yours, it's perfect for the American audience!"

I ended up, eventually, escaping from her and her continuous attempts to get me involved personally!

I couldn't be the main subject in this broadcast. It would have been unpleasant for the Benetton siblings if I had been, in such an important occasion for the Group, the official "Benetton" voice on air and steal the centre of stage!

In addition, they had their managing director, Aldo Palmeri, who came from Bank of Italy and had been the mind behind the Group's very successful floatation at the Milan stock exchange in 1985.

He was speaking a decent English and so I had taken the position that Aldo would have been the main Benetton spokesperson and the siblings would have been interviewed and directly answered in Italian, with English subtitles.

As a matter of fact, the part of interview where NBC went to Giuliana's office and main style and design department, with all her staff, became very famous because Giuliana, in perfect Venetian tradition, wasn't even speaking Italian, but our local dialect that sounded, to most, very funny!

The troupe went then to Rome, to complete the service and there the official company spokesperson was, in fact, Aldo Palmeri.

However, such was the insistence on her side that my voice should have come out somehow, that I had to accept to be interviewed at our Brentano's flagship store in 5th Avenue.

Eventually the Today's Show special on Benetton ended stating that we had been very effective with our marketing strategy, popping up with stores everywhere across the US, and that the special itself, had it been an advertising event commissioned by Benetton, would have costed us over $90 million.

The formula in the early years, was the key to success: a new Benetton store would generate a cash-flow that in just over six months repaid the initial investment. This would allow a geometrical expansion, since the owner would open a second store within one year, another two the following year and possibly other three or four the third year. This happened in many cases in Italy in the seventies and allowed some Benetton store owners to build up their companies to even twenty or thirty stores in a region, with very high profits.

Another new operation came to the horizon in 1985.

John, who was also involved with the agency that managed the area of north-east, told me that some developers were establishing a new concept in Freeport, Maine, where L.L. Bean was based.

I was familiar with the brand, but I had never been there, so we decided to go for a couple of days and see what it was all about.

We took a flight to Boston (in those years there was a shuttle service) and then drove to Freeport. I remember it was October, the peak season for the 'foliage', this incredible scenery of the woods changing colour with a variety of shades from green, to orange and yellow that really amazed me.

We visited L.L. Bean that had an independent building on three floors, each of approximately 5,000 sq. ft., and was declared 'open 24 hours a day for 365 days a year'!

They also had one of the largest catalogue sales businesses in US, with $300 million turnover and around 800 operators at a huge call-centre.

Well, I didn't believe this story about being 'open 24 hours a day', so I set my alarm for 4 am the following morning to personally pay them a visit.

To my surprise, not only did I find the store open, but there were about twenty cars in the car park, and quite a few people shopping inside! Amazing!

The interesting part was that, around this 'anchor', an open mall was being built, for 'Factory Outlet Stores', a totally new concept, nowadays well established everywhere.

John asked me if Benetton could have possibly been interested. I thought about it and said, "John, Benetton is manufacturing a total, including accessories, of 120 million pieces a year, and it's industrially physiological to have around 1.5% of defective goods coming out of production.

That means 1.8 million pieces a year. I know it's becoming an increasing problem for us. The only way to get rid of them, at a fraction of cost, is to negotiate with companies that are specialized in buying left over inventory or defective goods that in Italy we call *stockisti*.

They are a problem for several reasons: first, although we try to protect ourselves with contracts, you are never sure that they will sell these goods only in the agreed market and you can sometimes find some right in London or Paris, a terrible problem with our franchisees and for our general image."

I continued, "Secondly, they buy huge amounts but offer very little for these garments, normally $1 or 10% of your cost, and that means a considerable loss.

Let's say that the average industrial cost is $6, Benetton loses around $8/9 million a year on cost.

Here we have a possibility of selling these goods at a discount of 30% to 70% on Suggested Retail Price.

If I'm not wrong, Luciano might like the idea, it means saving $5 million a year and knowing for sure where the goods end.

Let me work on it and maybe we can do the retail operation together and make a nice profit. Luciano prefers his company not to be involved in retail directly."

After a couple of months, I brought Luciano over to Freeport where I had organized a meeting with the C.E.O. of L.L. Bean and we ended up opening the first Benetton Outlet a few months later, as well as signing a distributorship agreement for the brand <L.L. Bean> in Europe. Fantastic!

I formed a new company with the John and his brother which exclusively opened the outlets in USA, the first being in Freeport.

This store sold more than $1 million in the first two months of operation with peaks of 1,500 garments sold in one day over 2,500 square feet of retail area. On a yearly basis, we were selling over 200,000 pieces of Benetton stock!

In Italy they would not believe these figures, and Luciano and Gilberto were very happy to sell them to us for three times the price they were getting before.

In that period, I met another person who became a good friend: David Stern, a young lawyer that had been just appointed as "Commissioner" of the NBA.

Because Benetton owned the basketball team in Treviso that had just won the Italian championship, and Luciano's brother Gilberto was the president and a great basketball supporter, he was determined to convince the Benetton brothers to acquire a franchise in US.

We were continuously invited by him to various events, I remember a game at the Madison Square Garden between the New York Knicks of Patrick Ewing and the Boston Celtics of the great Larry Bird, Robert Parish, and Kevin McHale! Although the Celtics won the Eastern Conference that year, at Madison they lost 104 – 113 and it was a great battle! We were sitting right behind the side lane and on one occasion two players fell right into me and Luciano, throwing us away from our chairs!

After the match, David insisted we saw the locker rooms and how the after-match was being handled.

Our PR Sally was with us but, when we arrived at the door, David said to her "Unfortunately you are not allowed to enter!"

I ironically added, "Or were you hoping to get in, Sally?"

Benetton eventually never bought the franchise.

I went to some parties with David, in the following years and he was always available, very kind and not at all full of himself, although he had become a star, having proved to be the best Commissioner the NBA could get, and he went on for 30 years!

I saw him the last time, before he sadly passed away, in his office in New York; he was still a brilliant guy, we shared some nice memories, and I asked him to sign a photo of him, myself and my wife for my grandson.

In 1985 there was another event that I will always remember.

Fiorucci was having a great party where Madonna performed, and a few days before, one late afternoon, I was with Elio after a visit to the Fiorucci store; since I was with my car, when we finished, he said to me, "Let's go for a drink at Madonna's home, she is a nice girl!"

We went there, stayed for about an hour or so, with many friends in the loft. It was a lot of fun.

The night of the party, we had to meet at Studio 54 and when I arrived, around 10:30 pm, there was a huge crowd outside the entrance, with a couple of big bouncers tightly controlling the invitees.

I parked my car and, moving towards the entrance, I saw Elio sitting on some side steps in the dark, with a curious expression on his face.

I went to him and said, "Elio, what are you doing here? Why are you not inside?"

He answered, "I tried to get to the entrance, but the crowd wouldn't let me go through and so I thought to wait until somebody I knew would help me to get in."

"I can't believe it!" I said.

But he continued. "You know what? It has been an incredible experience for me! I have been able to quietly observe many people coming in, all of them are my clients, and I could observe them and their way of dressing, their way of walking and moving, talking, gesticulating, and all that while I was invisible to them. I have understood more in this hour or so, than with a very expensive market research!"

This was Elio Fiorucci, an intelligent, gentle, almost shy person, with a great mind!

Arrigo Cipriani had been a friend going back many years.

His father Giuseppe had opened the original Harry's Bar in Venice, where many artists and celebrities went, including Hemingway during the early 50s, who really made it an international destination.

Arrigo's son Giuseppe married Elisabetta, the daughter of a very famous Italian entrepreneur, Raul Gardini, who acquired the national giant chemical manufacturer Montedison.

With the help of Gardini, Arrigo, a very ambitious man, was soon negotiating with the Forte Group that had control over an incredible location in Central Plaza, right on the corner of the Sherry-Netherland Hotel.

Eventually Harry's Cipriani opened in November 1985 and was an immediate success.

It had reproduced the wonderful atmosphere of the Harry's Bar in Venice with a very similar decoration and menu.

But somebody didn't feel the same way: Brian Miller was one of the most authoritative restaurant critics in USA at the time and wrote an article on Harry's Cipriani giving an overall evaluation of 'mediocre'.

He criticised the food and stated that it was grossly overpriced!

Arrigo is a very proud man and doesn't take critics very easily, he thought that an American could not judge an Italian restaurateur with over 30 years of personal experience and, above all, a thousand years of cuisine tradition that was dating the glorious days of *La Serenissima Repubblica*, the empire of Venice that had a very strong culinary tradition.

So, he did what nobody else would have done: he took the back page of The New York Times (very expensive, I believe it was around $25,000 in those years) and wrote a letter to Miller contesting his criticism and basically asking him not to go back to his restaurant!

I personally believe that he was right, my full support was for Arrigo.

He had been very courageous to take this step; Miller was a powerful guy that could kill a restaurant at any time with a negative valuation and all the restaurateurs in NYC feared him! As a matter of fact, not much later Cipriani opened "Bellini" in the midtown west side and Giuseppe had already a great success with his Cipriani Downtown in West Broadway.

10

The Impossible Challenge: Brentano's and Wallis, the Southern States; The End of Benetton in the USA

Brentano's bookstore had been an icon in NYC since 1853 but unfortunately was finally liquidated in 1984 and the beautiful store was on the market for lease.

The Wallis family, once a powerful retail group in UK that also went through financial difficulties in late 70s, became a Benetton client in UK in early 80s.

The family sent Nick Wallis to NYC to possibly expand the Benetton business there with a megastore, since larger stores had always been their marketing strategy in UK.

Unfortunately, they didn't realize that Nick was more into parties than in the office. The property market was at its peak then and you would pay top rent for the best locations.

Nick secured the lease and went on to open the Megastore just at the time of my arrival. It was a suicidal move, as a franchisee, because there was no feasible proportion between rent paid and sales.

It lost money since day 1.

It was obvious that, sooner or later, probably sooner, the store would have to close and that was unacceptable, from our point of view, as overall image right at the time of our strong expansion in the US market!

I found myself in an almost 'Mission Impossible' situation: to convince Luciano that we had to buy the store out from Wallis at almost any cost, and run it as a direct 'flagship store' with Benetton USA.

Luckily, Wallis had a weak position in UK, because they were late with Benetton payments and risking of losing that business as well, and being his father Jeffrey in charge in UK, I had some margin of movement putting the two markets into one picture.

In the end I was able, after a very complicated and difficult negotiation, to achieve an agreement with the Wallis and Benetton, and Brentano's was saved!

It stayed our flagship store until October 1996 when Benetton opened the new one at the Scribner's building, acquired by the family.

In the meantime, the southern states were creating some problems to us: in general, the fashion awareness was much lower and so was the average disposable income, with the final effect that our garments were considered as too 'expensive'.

The Benetton agents involved were all young and flexible people, with basically nothing in their pockets, so they had approached their new position as "Benetton agent" with great enthusiasm and financial opportunity, since they were starting from zero!

But then we had a sudden problem with one of our agents, I'll call him "Mr. Z".

Luciano met him during a vacation in Sardinia. He liked this young and active waiter, even if a little rough in his manners and not certainly with a high education and asked him if he would be interested in a position in the USA.

Of course, Mr. Z showed immediate enthusiasm and Luciano sent him to London for a few months to get acquainted with the Benetton system and to learn a bit of English language that he didn't speak at all.

While in London, they sent him to an English school and, after a couple of months, he was proud to show improvements with the language.

So, one day the office staff wanted to order some food to be delivered, and Mr. Z said, "I'll call and order it!" They gave him the list and he called.

On the other side, somebody asked, "Who's speaking?"

He said, "Mr. Z, from the Benetton office, with Z as in Zebra."

The guy continued, "Can you spell it for me?"

Mr. Z went, "Z as in Zebra, E as in Eco, B as in boy, R as…" as the entire office started laughing like crazy.

One day, I received a call from one of our franchisees in Nashville, a well-known surgeon that had opened a Benetton store for his wife and was of course hoping to make at least some profit.

He was very distressed and insisted he had to personally talk to me, he wouldn't say anything over the phone.

He even sounded scared to me, so I decided to take the first flight and went.

We met secretly and he brought all sort of proof on what Mr. Z was doing to him and his wife: from asking a percentage on the interior decoration (unheard of, a shame!), to imposing very high initial budgets not justified by the scale of operation (Mr. Z was doing this only to increase his commissions, of course), to impose the quick opening of a second store, which meant another considerable investment without even knowing if the first one would never make a profit, probably not!

"Finally," he said, "he told me that if I hadn't done what he said, he would have taken away the operation from me at no cost and, if I talked to someone, he had some 'friends' that would take care of me and my wife."

That's why the poor guy was so scared.

I reassured him immediately, saying to him, "Wait until I intervene, it will happen very quickly. Do not mention anything, don't worry, he has no friends, he's bluffing to get you scared and so to force you to follow his impositions."

He thanked me a lot and I went back to NYC.

Luciano was arriving shortly, and I took the opportunity, one day we were going for lunch at the nearby 'Harry's Cipriani', to talk to him and inform him of the very serious situation.

Luciano had brought Mr. Z over to US, so I wanted him to approve we had to fire him on the spot and send him back to Italy, replacing his position, which we did immediately. It was one of the very few sad and embarrassing situations we ever experienced in many years, also because he acted almost as a *mafioso*.

I would like to say something about the Mafia. It is a reality in Italy and in particular in Sicily, where it started around 100 years ago.

I was always very curious to know if the popular stories about mafia and its way to do things was true or not.

I had an opportunity to find out with Michele, one of the most important Benetton clients in Palermo, whom I met going with Luciano at a private party near Bologna, where he was also invited.

After a few glasses of wine, when you loosen the tongue, I asked him if it was true that they paid the *pizzo*.

His answer was, "Well, until a few years ago, when we were directly paying the guys who had been sent by the family, the fortune was that we'd never need any present protection, whilst the guy was there.

"And, at the closing of the shops, it was sufficient a turn of key, without any security system or alarm, because any attempt of robbery would be punished by guys that don't send you their lawyer's threat of litigation, they break your knees! Nobody wants to confront that.

"Now that the state has taken control, with the police that should protect us, we had to install alarms, shutters, locks and so on and our life has become a nightmare!"

Another example of what the 'mafia' can do is about a Benetton area manager that had to visit the Palermo office. She had just received her brand-new BMW and was so excited that she asked Benetton if she could go with her own car, instead of the company's one, and be reimbursed on a kilometre basis. Benetton agreed and she went, the happiest girl in the world.

When she arrived in Palermo, she was directed by the office to the hotel where she had a reservation and parked her car in the hotel's secured car park.

The following morning, after breakfast, she went out, ready to go to the agency's office, when she suddenly realized, in a panic moment, that her car had been… stolen!

Desperate, she called the office and someone picked her up and a few minutes later she was, desperately crying, in front of Carmelo, our agent in Sicily.

Carmelo was short and bulky, with a round happy face and a funny attitude most of the time, and he was very gentle with girls, particularly the good-looking ones!

He asked her, with his strong Palermo's accent, "Darling, what's happened? Why are you crying?"

"Carmelo, I came with my brand new car and parked it at the hotel you reserved for me, but last night it was stolen!"

Carmelo thought for a moment and then took her under his arm and started to walk towards the showroom. "Don't worry, I'll make a few phone calls and see what I can do about it. You now work with my people on the new collection, and I want you to be happy and do the best you can in your job, I know you are very good at it. I'll see you later," he kissed her on the forehead and left.

A few hours later in the afternoon, she was taken back to the hotel, and, in absolute surprise, she found her car well washed, with a bunch of flowers on the driver's seat!

Incredulous, she asked the guy that gave her a lift from the office, "How is it possible? What happened?"

He answered with a smile, "Carmelo made a couple of calls to the right *picciotti*," (a Sicilian term for 'friendly mafiosi').

On the 19th of October 1987, there was one of the worst stock market crashes in history and the rate of exchange of Italian lira with the US dollar plummeted from Lit. 2,000 to Lit. 1,200, with the result that our prices went up by 65% compared to the beginning of our expansion back in 1984.

A basic example was the 'Polo Piquet', the classic polo shirt, which was originally at $7.50 to our stores and retailing at $19.90.

With the new rate in 1987 it went up to $12.40, retailing at $29.90 (up by 50%!). The situation was obviously dramatic with our store owners unable to make profit as before, and our main competitors taking advantage. We had to do something, and quickly.

I asked Flavio to search for some similar product we could outsource in Far-East, where he had some good contacts, and he came up with a very interesting prototype of the polo in plain colour at a cost, to us Benetton USA, of $3.40. That meant we could have sold it to our store-owners at $6.90 and a Suggested Retail Price of $19.90 with a multiplier on cost for the store of 2.9, better than the original 2.6.

We were enthusiastic and decided to involve some of the more important US Benetton agents to introduce the matter to Luciano at the first opportunity.

Luciano arrived 10 days later and found himself in an unexpected meeting with me, Flavio, John, Armando and a couple of others.

I broke the ice and said, "Mr. Luciano, we are going through a very difficult moment in collecting payments from the stores. Not only their sales are considerably down, but their margins are even worse, in essence the profitability of the Benetton operation in USA is at stake!" Flavio and the others immediately backed-up my introduction and expressed their fear we might go towards a dangerous period of difficulties, smaller orders and, ultimately, even stores' closures.

I then took out a of railing we had prepared, our polo at the existing retail price of $29,90 and some samples of our competitors (Gap, Banana Republic, Limited, etc.) that were ranging, for the same product, from retail prices of $9,90 to $14,90.

I then pulled out the sample form Korea that Flavio had found, and, with his help, we described all the positive aspects we could achieve by changing the supply to that source.

With our total surprise, Luciano was aggressively negative, telling us, "I don't think the difference in price is the reason for our negative performance. People appreciate the quality of 'Made in Italy', which we have always taken as a proud flag of our collection, and the materials we use with it, not the cheap one you show me from Far East. The reality is that you are not doing your job properly, the management of the stores is not adequate, so is the merchandising and window dressing and, above all, you are letting your clients buy what they want in the collection, instead of guiding them professionally to proper orders, both in terms of mix of product and quantities.

"In fact, I can announce that we have decided to buy a factory in Rocky Mount, North Carolina, where we'll shortly start production of a list of classic cotton styles. This will allow us, saving on import custom-duties, to sell at much better prices to our store owners, thus improving their margin, as you require. Nevertheless, I insist you look deeply into your operation and staff, both in the office and stores, because I have recently seen a very low standard!"

We were all shocked by his reaction, and wondered what we could have done to make him change his mind!

Whatever we did, in the near future, didn't work, and the new factory in Rocky Mount was a useless attempt: Carlo Benetton had sent one of his loyal managers to run the operation, with the precise instruction to maximize the factory's profit, not to help the store owners in difficulty!

So, what happened was that all the line of classics, now 'Made in the USA', was an average 8 % cheaper than the original Italian price, and such a small reduction had no effect on our stores' profitability.

The result was a massacre among the 750 US stores, which started to close down, in a spiral, in the next two to three years.

I had foreseen this coming, and I asked Luciano to relinquish my agency in Manhattan, with the objective of concentrating in the Middle East and UK, where my direct involvement had become necessary.

In the meantime, I had already arranged for a substitute in Benetton USA, where my job had been completed and now needed only a good manager for the necessary follow-up. Our H.R. dept found the right candidate in Federico Minoli, a guy with whom I developed a good relationship during his take-over.

In the end, however, Luciano was very rigid in evaluating economically my business in NYC, the Manhattan agency and the stores we owned with B&A. The difference from what the stores owned of delivered merchandise to Benetton Group and the little value Luciano gave, resulted in almost a $1 million that I would have to pay to exit the market.

I remember a telephone conversation between myself in NYC and Luciano in Treviso when, at a certain point, he almost shouted at me, "You keep talking of selling your business, but you have nothing to sell, your agency and stores belong to Benetton, the trademark is ours and you have nothing to sell!"

I then couldn't refrain myself from responding, "In this case, Mr. Luciano, if you believe that after all I have done for you and your company in the last ten years is worth nothing, okay, I will pay the money you want. But I am herewith immediately resigning from all my positions. Please ask the administrative department to prepare the final account with me and my companies (I still had thirteen Benetton stores in the UK), we'll settle at the first opportunity, and I'll go on my way."

This abruptly concluded our telephone conversation and I started to pack my things to leave, once for all, the United States.

I certainly had a bitter taste in my mouth, I was sad and disappointed for two reasons: the first, I would have expected more flexibility from the family, if not for the fact that I had made an excellent investment for them. When I arrived, we had a lease at the General Motors building for only 2,500 sq. ft. of office space.

After just one year we obviously needed a much bigger place and I suggested to Gilberto that, rather than paying a rent for no benefit, not even fiscal, we could have bought a freehold in a new building.

Gilberto was not convinced, but I insisted that the Real Estate market in would go quickly up and that having the liquidity in Benetton Group, there was no financing cost either. At the end he agreed, and we bought for $8 million, with Benetton USA, an entire 6,000 sq. ft. floor on 59th St., between Madison and Park Avenue, a beautiful location that Gilberto sold around 10 years later for over $50 million!

The second and more important reason was that I knew that this decision of following the path of all American brands that were leaving US for manufacturing purposes, setting up their own operation in far East, would be vital for the existence of our network in USA.

Continuing with the stubborn supply of "Made in Italy" products, for which in effect nobody cared for a brand at our level, would have caused most of our stores to go, sooner or later, out of business.

It was a big disappointment for me to see that nobody, not even Luciano, foresaw the gravity of this.

At the end, I left USA by the end of 1991 when the stores were still almost 700, but by 1995 they had dropped to just 150.

I then went to Dubai to prepare for all the rest to be liquidated. Chiara was concerned not only for our future, we had to re-create ourselves somehow, but also because we might have had to leave Dubai, and she loved the place.

However, soon after our arrival, Gianni, the head of Administration, a friend of mine since well before our Benetton experience, called me and "Francesco, I spoke to Luciano this morning. He is very sad for what happened and told me that we cannot lose a man of your level, quality and loyalty, and so he invited me to call you and try anything possible to convince you to stay."

"Gianni, thanks for your effort, but it's too easy to tell me that Benetton appreciates me, but I have to pay, in full, $1 million without any compensation of any kind!"

"No – he quickly interrupted me – I have changed his mind on this, here is the proposal: we give you only a small discount on the outstanding merchandise in NYC, but I'll help you to sell your operation in UK, and this is pre-approved by Luciano, including the stores, at a fair price. We have already one of the agents there, Piero, who agrees with us to take over, at our terms.

For whatever difference you had to pay, and it shouldn't be much, we'll finance you from Milan for five years at zero interest. What do you think? Come on! It's a good proposal, I had to throw myself to the floor in front of Luciano to get you this, but he was also, I must say, very well oriented to accept because he recognizes the great job you have done in US and he thinks you are one of the best, if not the best, managers he has had in Benetton. What do you say?"

After remaining silent for a few seconds, I then answered "OK, Gianni, I think it's a fair proposal, thank you for your effort, I accept and will be ready to sign all the necessary paperwork when you have it."

"One last thing – he added – Luciano wants me to tell you that you both have to turn the page and look to the future with the same enthusiasm you had back in 1984:"

That, I must confess, pleased me because it wasn't easy to be given a clear sign of appreciation from Luciano.

11

Luciano and the Underdog Zara, Giuliana and the Wrong Tip, Mauro and Afef

In 1988, during one of my days dedicated to examining what our competitors were doing, which new products or marketing strategies were being brought into the fashion business, I noticed a new store had just opened in Lexington Avenue & 54th St. It was an unknown, to me, Spanish retailer called ZARA.

I carefully visited the store, a few times, and convinced myself that it had some potential, even though the product was basic and rough, not very sophisticated, but at a very competitive retail price level.

The thing that more impressed me was the peculiar way to label the garments with paper tickets that were carrying several retail prices of different countries in Europe and, of course, the USA.

Now, the interesting thing was that, if you took the rate of exchange out of the picture, the price was identical!

If a sweater was, for example, $29 in NYC, it was the equivalent converted at the rate of exchange in French Francs in Paris, or in UK pounds in London and so on.

That didn't make sense if you considered shipping costs, eventual custom duties, different operating expenses such as rent, salaries, local taxes, etc. To maintain the same gross profit performance, retail prices had to vary.

That meant that there was a deliberate strategy behind this, to strongly fix in the customer's mind the image that Zara was a competitive brand, very reasonably priced, everywhere! Weather you bought it in London, Paris or elsewhere, didn't make any difference.

This was a very intelligent approach, since it was giving up some margin to a more valuable, long-term image!

I considered this a very smart and forward-looking view.

When Luciano arrived in NYC next, I took him to visit anonymously the Zara store, and underlined my impression as I stated above.

To my surprise, he totally dismissed the case, telling me, "This is not a proper retail operation. If they really operated like this, they would be bankrupt very soon, it's all *uno specchietto per le allodole!*" (an Italian sentence that translates, I believe, in 'smoke and mirrors', meaning a trick to attract somebody's attention or an illusion).

Well, even geniuses make mistakes. Luciano, in this underestimation of Zara, was wrong!

There have been various attempts to explain the difference between the two competitors, Benetton, and Zara, but in my view it's very simple: it's the retail formula.

The Benetton so called 'franchise' system (technically it isn't, it's a license, but that it's too complicated and boring) was a definite advantage in the early stages: the perfect example is in fact our rapid expansion in the USA!

If you have interested investors, you don't need any auto-financing since the necessary capital is brought by them and this speeds up exponentially your development in the market.

On the contrary Zara, who was only operating directly owned stores, and started in Spain in the same mid-sixty's years, had to go very slowly at the beginning when they were a small retailer and needed financing for any further expansion.

We all know how difficult it is for a small company to have access to a third-party financing, particularly with the banking system.

But, assuming the same good level of operation, in terms of product, quality, customer service and so on, in the long-term Zara's advantage has been obvious: a more consistent image but, above all, a much more competitive retail price!

The final situation is that when I went to NYC our consolidated Benetton turnover was approx. $4 billion and Zara was much smaller. Now Benetton turnover is just $1 billion and Inditex, Zara's Holding company, is positioned at $18 billion! What do you think, had Luciano underestimated his rival?

Giuliana had always been strictly involved with the product. She was not really a stylist, nor a designer, but she had an incredible gift to understand immediately if a certain style that anyone of her staff suggested, during the creation of a new collection, would fit or not.

And, if it didn't, she could put her finger on the small wrong detail and immediately find the way to correct it.

All of this always, invariably, speaking Venetian dialect!

She's been in New York only once, with a couple of her assistants, for two or three days in 1986. She came to finally see the "Big Apple" and what was the fashion world proposing there.

The last evening, we went for dinner at the famous Chinese restaurant "Mr. Chow" and the food was, as usual, excellent.

At the end, I asked for the check and the manager on duty brought it to me, I gave him my credit card, the ' Benetton USA" one, and we waited for the printed voucher to sign.

Giuliana was sitting next to me and, when the check arrived, I knew she would be very aware of the total amount; after all, she was the sister of her brothers, and she couldn't be different in not liking to spend money easily!

The tradition was, in NYC, to double the tax (which was 8.25 %) to leave the correct tip, approx. 17%.

I knew very well she couldn't understand and accept a tip of that magnitude, since in Italy very few people leave a tip in the first place, and, even if they do, surely nothing more than 10%!

So, for once, with the check at $1,200, I left $50 tip, instead of the usual $200.

The waiter took the plate with the check, and after a few moments the manager on duty came back and said to me loudly "Was there anything wrong, Mr. Della Barba? I see the tip you left, and I wonder if…"

"Oh yes!" I said, interrupting him. "I made a mistake; can you please reprint the voucher and I'll change it."

He left with a satisfied expression on his face.

Giuliana didn't speak any English, and barely Italian, so she asked me what had happened with the check, and I just told her there was something wrong with it.

When the manager came back, having torn the previous voucher and with the new one, on the blank space for the gratuity I put 'zero' and closed the check with the actual amount of the invoice, without any tip at all, and then added, with an angry voice, "Now the check is right! Remember that a tip is a voluntary gesture that a client may leave if inclined to do so, it is by no means an obligation! So, shame on you for what you told me and don't dare doing that again, with me, ever!"

He left, red in his face and embarrassed, and Giuliana was very curious to know what happened.

Only at that point I told her the full story and their complaint about the $50 tip.

I then went on with the grand finale that I left no tip at all and shouted to the manager never to do that again.

With a big smile she said, "Well done, Francesco, you're absolutely right, this is exaggerated and not at all the conduct a manager should have!"

I knew that deep inside, she was happy, because I was not lightly spending 'her' money, and from that moment I became a hero in her eyes!

As I already said, Luciano and his brothers and sister have always been, let's say, meticulously careful about spending money!

Having said that, they have naturally used these principles in their kids' education as well! At the beginning, I thought it was right and very respectable that they taught their kids never to be showing off, or spending silly amounts for silly things, maybe to just amaze friends.

There are too many Italian youngsters, ignorant and arrogant, who go around in sport cars with expensive Rolex watches and burn their parents' money like idiots!

These are the ones who normally destroy any good business their father might have built with hard work and dedication when, still young, they are wrongly put in charge of the business by their same father who is not able to judge if they are capable and ready to take the position. Big mistake.

On the other hand, if your parents tell you, since your early age, "Be aware, you'll have plenty of so-called friends that will surround you only because you are a 'Benetton', and they will be looking for you to pay the bill! Do not fall in this trap, don't offer freely anything, let them pay for you, if they are really friends!"

Well, it's difficult to become a normal person, even if you are smart!

In 1993 Mauro, the older one, started suddenly a love-story with Afef, a beautiful model originally from Tunisia who had been married to a well-known lawyer and businessman in Rome.

The couple was stunning, both beautiful and young, and they were at the centre of attention wherever they went.

Once in Treviso we were invited, with Luciano, at a home party given by one of the business associates of Benetton, the manufacturer of all the Benetton shopping bags who, of course, had made a fortune himself.

There were around 40 invitees, I was chatting with my wife Chiara, Luciano, and his close friend Massimo, in Treviso nicknamed 'Dr. Sorzòn'. On this, I must expend a few words: Massimo was a tall, handsome guy, as stingy as Luciano, and became his close friend, being invited by Luciano several times to travel on his private jet around the world. Massimo had a small company producing rat poison and he was very smart and fast to take advantage of being with Luciano and getting interviewed as well, everywhere they went, claiming he had killed all the rats in NY, and other major cities. All of this was grossly inflated to get himself a good publicity. Now, the common friends who knew him in Treviso, since in Venetian dialect the word 'rat' is *sorze* instead of the Italian *Topo*, they called him ironically 'Dr. Sorzòn' or the 'Doctor Terminator' of all rats!

Going back to the party, suddenly Mauro and Afef arrived and the entire crowd in the room stopped, in silence, to look at the two beautiful people walking in.

Afef had a diamond ring on her finger that was probably fifteen carats or so, a beautiful and very, very expensive diamond that was shining so strongly in all directions that we felt we almost had to put our sunglasses on!

Suddenly, Luciano got closer to Massimo and, lowering his voice, asked "Mauro didn't buy that diamond for Afef, right?" very worried about the amount Mauro could have spent in such case!

Dr. Sorzòn reassured him immediately, "Don't worry, Luciano, that's a present from her previous husband, the lawyer in Rome."

Luciano had a sigh of relief, and we went on with the party!

Several years later, Massimo had an acute attack of back hernia, very painful and he couldn't even move from his bed.

After consultation, it was decided he needed urgently an operation and wanted to go to one of the best surgeons in Paris.

Luciano promptly offered his jet to transport the poor guy on a stretcher to the Paris private aviation section and then immediately to the hospital.

The surgery was successful, and after a couple of weeks Massimo came back home to Treviso, where he found a nice surprise: an invoice from 'BenAir', the company that was managing the three jets that Benetton Group had, of which I don't remember the exact amount, more or less €6,500!

He immediately called Luisa, Luciano's secretary, asking her what was this all about, how was it possible that Luciano had approved to make him pay for the flight?!

She candidly answered "Massimo, these are the instructions Luciano gave me, to give exceptionally a 50% discount off the normal flight rate!"

Call it friendship!

12

Luciano's Interview at Mixer and Giuliana's Portrait by Andy Warhol

In early 1985 our PR office in Ponzano received a request from RAI, the National TV broadcast, for the participation of Luciano Benetton at a TV show greatly followed, in those days, called 'Mixer' and run by Giovanni Minoli.

It was the first Italian attempt for a talk show face-to-face between the journalist and various celebrities.

Benetton was the name on everyone's lips at that time, following the extraordinary financial results and the quotation of the Benetton shares at Milan stock exchange.

It was predictable that Luciano would be one of the candidates for the new broadcast.

However, there was a certain concern regarding the capability of Luciano to properly answer delicate questions and, in general, he wasn't the best speaker in the world.

As a matter of fact, he had already been at elocution lessons organized by our PR department, mainly, at the beginning, to minimize the typical venetian accent immediately recognizable by anybody outside Veneto.

We talk, particularly in our dialect, with a strong 'monotone' for which we are often ridiculed by Italians of other regions.

At the end the interview was anyway confirmed, and Luciano went to RAI 3.

Overall, the interview went well, but there was a critical moment when all of us held our breath because this was the exchange:

Minoli – Mr. Luciano, we all know how successful you have been around the world, and this must have taken a lot of hard work, long hours of traveling and so on, was it very hard for you?

Luciano – Not really, for me visiting our clients and our shops is an enjoyment, discovering that a new shop is doing well and how we can contribute to make it perform even better, is part of my life and I do it happily.

Minoli – But… what is really more important for you, your work or your family?

(Here there is a very important detail: in the Italian language, *il* is masculine, while *la* is feminine. Minoli's question in Italian was *"Per lei, è più importante il lavoro o la famiglia?"* This because *lavoro* is masculine and *famiglia* is feminine).

Luciano's answer was, almost immediately, "Naturalmente il… (here he stopped a couple of seconds and added) lavoro richiede molto impegno, ma le soddisfazioni della famiglia sono impagabili."

Translated, "Naturally business requires hard work and commitment, but the satisfaction that family gives you is priceless."

Now, had he wanted to say that family was more important, he would have started saying "Naturalmente la…"

But everybody on our side understood very well that he was spontaneously answering, "Naturalmente il lavoro!" (Naturally my business") but realizing this would have been controversial and unpopular, he corrected himself just in time to say that the family was really the most important value!

Basically, a very good last minute turn, in his response, that saved possible controversy and kept his image 'politically correct' to the public's eye.

Watching the interview on TV, live, at Benetton we all had a sigh of relief!

More or less at the same time, in 1986, I received a call from our PR department.

In 1983 Benetton had acquired Calzaturificio di Varese, an old manufacturer of shoes in Varese (north of Milan) which was closing down.

It was a very convenient price for Benetton and there was a good brand name that could have been combined with the more modern style and fashion research of Benetton.

Above all, the Benetton line could have been completed with proper shoes, planned and produced internally, instead of the very limited selection of shoes outsourced here and there, generally available in our stores.

Our PR thought that it would have been a great publicity and marketing tool if the shoebox had been properly personalized with some colourful and unequivocally recognizable Benetton detail.

I do not remember exactly who had the brilliant idea to get a portrait of Giuliana Benetton made by the most famous pop artist at that time: Andy Warhol.

Anyway, so it went, and I was instructed to organize the entire thing, from contacting Andy, negotiating a compensation that had to be inclusive of 'commercial rights of the image', given the usage we had in mind, and finally completing the process required.

It was an exciting adventure, since Andy was a peculiar person and he was pleasant in his approach but discontinue in his behaviour and therefore difficult to manage, particularly since Giuliana was not certainly available to become a model for an extended period of time.

At the end the portrait was somehow made, and we had a big party with a press conference that presented the painting and the prototype of the shoebox that would have had Giuliana's image on the side.

The painting was oil on canvas and was really beautiful and eventually consigned to Giuliana in person.

It has been a great upset for me to know, a few years later, that Giuliana had actually sold the portrait, and I do not know for which reason, it could not be the money, of course.

But I would have never sold it had I have been… in her shoes!

13

Parkinson Disease and my Antidote, the Love of My Life.

In 1989, my life was going through, once again, a violent turmoil.

I had my second separation in the middle of 1988, with two beautiful daughters, 8- and 3-year-old, and they were living with their mother in Milan. Although I was seeing them regularly, of course I was missing them and carrying a strong sense of guilt.

But it was inevitable, the relationship with my second wife had become unbearable and dangerous, since we were both almost physical in our fights, and this was not good for anybody, in particular for the girls.

I had already made this choice years before, when I decided that my life was more precious than anything else and that I would keep alive, in my heart, the dream of finding the real "Love" rather than accepting to live a quiet, unhappy life, like most people do.

We have a sentence in Italy that says, "La Fortuna aiuta gli audaci" ("Good luck helps the audacious or intrepid") meaning that if you don't look for something you really want, if you don't take your chances and risks, luck will not help you.

I was going back to Treviso at the end of November 1988 and, as a coincidence, it was my birthday too, so I organized a small party with some friends. My brother came with a friend, a beautiful girl, that immediately caught my attention.

Chiara had a model's *physique du rôle* (she had in fact been modelling before), curly dark long hair and beautiful blue eyes, exactly my type!

We started to talk a lot, that evening, and she told me she was working with the regional representative office of Armani and other high fashion brands, being responsible for marketing and sales.

She immediately sounded to me a smart, sharp, and interesting person, full of curiosity for anything new, with a lovely character.

Coming out of a tumultuous relationship that had lasted nine years, it was like a dream come true for me!

Nothing happened, but I was determined to see her again and when I came back from New York for Christmas and spent a couple of weeks in Treviso, our relationship started, but was almost compromised, right at the beginning.

She had second thoughts, mainly because of my past: two weddings and four children were a bit too much and she decided to stop seeing me. She told me so at lunch, one of those days, and I was devastated because I was already madly in love with her.

I went back to my hotel, and started to think about it, and decided that I would not accept to lose her without even trying to see if we could have a relationship.

I called her back and gently insisted, for a couple of days, that we should have talked about us some more, before giving up, and I promised that I didn't want to force anything, just a better understanding of each other.

She must have been shaky as well in her decision, because she accepted to see me, and we eventually fell completely in love with each other.

The 12th of January 1989 became our day, we still celebrate the date as our anniversary, but a few days before we had a funny episode: it was late in the evening, around midnight, and we were slowly driving in my Jeep Cherokee (a beautiful old model of 1978 , with 3 gear transmission and 5 litre engine) with the official Marlboro colours (it belonged to a friend of mine in Milan who had the Marlboro F1 racing team in the 70s and who sold it to me).

I said that I was thirsty and launched the idea that the only place where we could drink something during the week was at the Cipriani Hotel in Asolo, where we could have taken a room and gotten the room service…

It was an awkward attempt to take her to bed and she rightly laughed at me and said, "Don't you have anything better? Come on, take me home."

While I was driving her back home, she suddenly asked me, "Where did you get your tie?" with an inquisitive look that gave me the impression of jealousy and disbelief.

"It's a present from a friend of mine, why?"

"Is it the sales assistant?"

Her look, tone of voice and face where all referring, with disgust, to a beautiful girl who worked at one of the best stores in Treviso, and whom she knew very well.

In reality, what she was really asking was whether I had had an affair with the girl. Which I had. I quickly tried to find a way out of this confrontation.

So, I looked at her and immediately said, "Why? You don't like it? Me neither." Saying this, I started to untie it, opened the window, and threw it away.

She smiled amused and confessed, later, that that gesture had made me gain her esteem and sympathy.

I was so in love with her, and I still am, that I would have done anything to stay with her, even a few moments.

I was extremely busy with my position in US, nevertheless I was capable of taking a flight to Rome on Friday night, arrive Saturday morning, stay with her in Rome for two days and fly back to New York on Sunday night!

I have lived the happiest life on earth ever since, she eventually became best friend with my daughters as well, and we always repeat to ourselves that we have been extremely lucky to find each other, a fortune that belongs to very few persons.

Life has been tough, sometimes, as it always is for almost everybody, and in 2010, when I was diagnosed with Parkinson, it seemed like the world would collapse on us.

In fact, after the diagnosis, an English specialist in London told me "If I were you, I wouldn't start a business with a five-year plan or go around the world in a sailboat alone," meaning that my deterioration would have probably been fast and compromising my overall abilities, in particular physical balance.

At that point my future looked very uncertain and, on suggestion of a good friend of mine, an Italian researcher and Professor at Yale University, Sandro Santin, I went to Columbia University Parkinson Center in NY, where I met Dr. Stanley Fahn, considered one of the founders of modern neurology in Parkinson since the 70s and who received many International and US awards for his studies and trials on PD.

A very gentle person who really impressed me since our first meeting. His assistants thoroughly examined me for over two hours, and he came into the picture the last 45 minutes, getting all the details and then personally conducting the last tests. I remember when he asked me to stand with my legs apart and invited me to try to resist his attempt to make me lose my balance.

He came from the back and pushed me forward but, being myself much taller and stronger than him, the result was that he almost lost his balance backward and smiling he said, "You are very strong!"

He completely changed the medical flowsheet I had been given in London and introduced Selegiline, a very important factor for me.

However, he did not say anything conclusive at the end of our first meeting and, since I was living in Italy, he gave me another appointment in one year time.

Only after my second visit he concluded, having seen that I hadn't changed much, "You are a mild case, I think with the right medication you will be able to cope with PD quite well."

He invited me to live an active life and to exercise physically, which I have always done in my life, being a lover of all sports and activities.

Name one, I have at least tried it: from skying to tennis, from fencing to track-and-field, from scuba-diving to windsurfing, from bowling to boxing, and many others to, last but not least, golf, where I have been an avid player for 30 years.

As an amateur, I have a personal record of 85 victories in local tournaments around the various countries where I lived and played.

Right before the diagnosis I had gone back to boxing training during my usual stay in Miami, in early spring. I had enjoyed boxing as an amateur while I was younger.

I went to the 5th Street Gym, the glorious original Angelo Dundee's gym where Muhammed Ali started his career when he was fifteen. The place is still full of pictures of that era.

After Angelo, it went to his children who eventually sold it and it was run, when I started, by Dino, an Italian American who contributed to make boxing training popular among the best models in Miami.

He was personally training Adriana Lima who, by the way, was very fast and had a good technique. When she was coming with a few of her colleagues, the entire gym would stop, fascinated by these beauties punching and sweating between themselves.

A few years later an international study on PD patients concluded that 'boxing training' was one of the best exercises because it was stimulating the hand-eye coordination and so, I discovered of having been a precursor.

The main ingredient of my having been able to fight Parkinson, however, was Chiara, my perfect companion who has been always at my side, encouraging me when necessary, pushing me if I had a moment of discouragement and always sharing with me both happiness and pain. She knows me so well that she can feel every miniscule emotion, either positive or negative, that I experience and therefore acts accordingly, with love, in our best interest.

I could not, sincerely, have dreamed of a better woman in my life and I always tell her that, without her, I would not be here and who I am today.

We still feel that all in all, we have been very lucky with our life, having a business that allowed us to travel around the world and meet new people and countries, new mentalities and cultures, and we've always been open-minded and attracted by the different.

We recently checked, out of curiosity, and discovered that we have been in one third of all the 250 countries in the world, not bad as travellers!

In this respect I am proud of myself, and I think to deserve it, because I never give up, I consider Parkinson as a bad companion in my life, who must fight very hard to beat me, until the last day.

14

Gino Pilota: an Intermittent Star in the Benetton Sky

I met him in the early 80s, immediately after starting with Benetton, when I was the 'new kid on the block' and he was one of the founders of Benetton business, greatly loved and hated, but always a bit envied for his success and money.

He liked me, probably because I was exuberant and would contribute to make 'fun and noise' if there was any opportunity of doing so, particularly at a bar or disco, with nice girls.

But who was Gino? He came from Pescara, a town in the middle of Italy, in Abruzzo, right on the Adriatico coast.

With only 120,000 inhabitants, similar to my Treviso, with the same provincial attitude of trying to know all the important people and talk a lot about anyone.

Gino was one of the very early clients of Luciano and became one of his best friends since the beginning.

Although very different in character and attitude with life: Gino was loud, a big spender, gambler and womanizer, the opposite of Luciano.

But, in Luciano's view, he had some great qualities: he was a shrewd businessman, and he would do anything for Luciano and Benetton.

He first gained Luciano's respect and trust, that would make his fortune, when Luciano went to Pescara in the early 70s and confessed to Gino that they were in trouble.

He supplied some German retailers from Monaco with a substantial delivery of goods, on credit, who apparently sold the goods very well, reordering them in bigger quantities, but suddenly not paying promptly as promised, and he and Gilberto were worried about the situation.

Gino immediately said to Luciano "Give me the name and address of these clients and I will get the money for you!"

Luciano commented "Why, do you know the German market?" and Gino replied "don't worry about that, just give me the list."

So, he did, and Gino went to Monaco.

Don't think that he knew anybody in Monaco or that he had some other solution.

He simply brought with him a couple of that kind of friends that you would not want to see angry with you and to whom you wouldn't want to owe any money.

With them he went around the various clients and, miraculously, he came back a week later with all the outstanding amounts, in cash!

Of course, their personal visit must have been very convincing!

Luciano and Gilberto didn't know the details, which Gino had kept for himself, but were very happy about the outcome and Luciano, when Gino expressed the intention of getting personally responsible for the development of the Benetton business in Germany, immediately agreed and so the story started.

Shortly, Germany became a very strong market and Luciano, as usual, decided that the country had to be divided into a few representative areas, which he did.

But here Gino made his brilliant move: for the first time, he suggested to Luciano the idea that the German market, very difficult to manage, needed a 'supervisor' like him to function properly. Such a 'supervisor', to cover the costs of his activity, needed a commission of 2%, while the local agents would have made the normal commission of 5%.

He was, at the end, agent in Monaco and Baviera, and supervisor for Germany.

A few years later, in the early 80s, Benetton had reached a turnover of €75 million in Germany, therefore Gino was receiving about €1,5 million a year just as 'supervisor'! No wonder he had a private plane and was living the life of a millionaire!

One of the crucial moments that cemented their friendship was in late seventies, when Gino was already established in Germany, where he was making important profits, but still hadn't reached his top levels.

The political situation in Italy was very unstable, these were the famous *anni di piombo*, when Red Brigades and extreme leftists were a daily nightmare, and the entire industrial sector was experiencing a ferocious social battle between the private companies and their workers and unions' officials.

Strikes, disruption of work, absenteeism and picket lines were daily news, and it became increasingly difficult for all industries to cope with this.

Benetton was under scrutiny of unions because of their network of small individual independent factories below the critical number of fourteen employees, which were not directly controllable by unions!

This smart solution created by the Benetton group, was now under fierce attack of CGIL, CISL and UIL, the three powerful unions in Italy, who coordinated strong picket lines in Ponzano.

Benetton was for the first time in financial difficulty, to the extent of risking closing down because of the loss of sales during the strikes, and the lack of strength with the banking system (these were the 70s and Benetton was not yet the strong cash machine that became later).

Banks wouldn't support, little sales coming through, Luciano and Gilberto didn't know what to do: their company was, for the first and only time, in danger of closing down!

But then, suddenly, there came a big help that nobody expected. Gino Pilota said to the brothers, "Here I am, I made good money because of you, I have important savings and they are all for you in this critical moment, you will pay me back when we'll be able to come through this crisis. If it doesn't work, and we fail, nothing changes for me: I didn't have any money before and will not have any money after! I'm fine!"

Eventually, history shows that the intervention was successful, and the two Benetton brothers never forgot the generosity of the only person that put his own wealth and life at stake to help them, and this explains also why they have accepted from Gino things and events that they would have never accepted by anybody else.

In the meantime, Gino was getting richer, and had expanded his business in other countries as well: he was present in Brazil, country that he loved and where he had many friends, and in Paris, where he had opened a very important megastore mainly to please Luciano, since in Paris nobody had had the courage for such an experiment, given the very high operating expenses.

The store was not doing as well as he expected, and he was starting to think how to make Luciano accept that he eventually closed it down. Very difficult task, because closing a store was, for Luciano, like killing a baby! He wouldn't take it!

Fortunately for Gino, destiny came in play for him: he was in Pescara one late afternoon when he received an urgent call from the young lady that was responsible at the Paris Megastore and who told him, in full panic, "Mr. Pilota, we have a fire going on, it started in the basement storage, probably where the electric circuits are! We are starting now to bring all the goods from the basement upstairs, while we wait for the firefighters!"

"Listen to me very carefully," he answered with a lower-tone angry voice. "Instruct all the staff to immediately bring all the goods from the retail floor to the storage!"

When she tried to react with, "But... sorry... I don't understand..." he stopped her and screamed, "Do exactly as I told you and shut up!"

Eventually the Megastore was unfortunately closed because of a devastating fire and Gino collected the full cost of his ordered goods from the insurance...

His natural character was taking over: he was slightly arrogant, at times very arrogant, when drunk (which happened more frequently with time passing by) he was almost violent, and big gambler in all the major European casinos, where he was well known and had substantial lines of credit.

I have never seriously played in casinos, I occasionally went with friends to have fun for a couple of hours, always starting with a small amount of money (let's say €500) and considering this money already lost (I never expected to win).

That was, in my view, the only possible way to approach gambling, otherwise you are dead.

It happened to me only once to be present with Gino in a casino, in Austria for a F1 Grand Prix in Zwelteg (he was a good friend of Senna), around 1983 or 84, I'm not sure.

I was shocked to see him playing at the roulette: he would only want to play on his own at the table (that's why he was playing mostly in Privee) and would only play the *vicini dello zero* (neighbours of zero), the 16 numbers between 22 and 25, including the 'zero'.

But he was really playing mainly the numbers 32 (by far his favourite), and the two on each side of the 32, numbers 15 and 19, and 0 (zero) and 26.

And he was playing increasing betting, didn't matter if he was winning or losing, becoming more and more aggressive, which translated either in big wins or big losses!

Given the 'law of large numbers', the gambler ends up losing his pants.

That night Gino lost (a considerable amount of money, but nothing more than normal, probably the equivalent of €40/50,000 today), and we then left for a drink in a night club.

Let's take into consideration an example for each category of results: a big win and a big loss.

An example of big win was once in Monte Carlo, when with his good friend Piero, he ended at 6 am (in the morning!) having won about €1 million! They were also drunk, with the company of five or six beautiful girls, and left the casino with a briefcase of cash.

They decided it was a glorious day in the summer, and that they should go out at sea for a day of sunshine, swim, and fun with the girls. What they needed was a boat or, better, a yacht, given their habitual levels!

So, they went to the marina and, as soon as it was opened, they bought (not rented! Bought!) a second-hand yacht for approx. 7/800 thousand euros and required immediately a skipper to take them out.

Whoever sold the boat to them, must have thought that they were crazy (actually drunk crazy…) and got them the first available yacht captain that accepted to get them out straight away for cash.

It must not have been a good one, because when they came back in the afternoon, probably not familiar with the local sea level, he hit a rock, he ripped open the yacht which eventually sank.

Since they didn't have any insurance (remember? They got out in a rush!) the yacht and its value were totally lost.

Never mind, we'll win another one!

The big loss example is unfortunately of public knowledge:

In 1991, Gino played, as usual, alone against the casino in San Remo, where he had a credit line of €1 million, in a private room with some friends.

He went on a losing spiral heavier than usual, and he was unfortunate that the usual manager was not there.

There was an unknown manager on duty that, probably uncertain on how to behave with a famous client of the casino that was begging and screaming for more credit, instead of stopping him after the loss of the first €1 million, kept giving him more and more credit, until the loss reached the value of 8 billion Italian lire, the equivalent toady of at least €6 million!

Of course, Gino was on all the newspapers and TV reports the following morning, and the Benetton found themselves at the centre of interest of all major newspapers and naturally denied any interview or comments, but I know that both Gilberto and Luciano were very disturbed by this event, which discredited them to the eyes of the public, with one of their top agents involved in such a scandal!

They decided, for the first time in their life, that it was now the moment to force Gino Pilota to retire and this was, for him, the beginning of the end: he died in 2008 in his native Pescara, poor and forgotten, after living the life of a star.

15

Flying: A Love Affair and a Duty, Gilberto and the Parallel Market

Flying has been always a pleasure and a passion for me. Some people are understandably terrified by the idea of catching a plane and are even more so if, unfortunately, there is a turbulent flight, when the airplane shakes or even jumps up and down!

To me, it has always been an exciting experience, not a scary one!

It was Christmas of 1995 and I had already left the USA for Dubai, where in 1989 I had moved my Middle East office for Benetton, and I was regularly going back and forth between the two offices.

Consider that moving around in the Middle East is impossible by car, so every time you need to be somewhere else, even a neighbouring country like Qatar, very close to Dubai, you must take a plane.

Kim, my secretary in UK, informed me that my office was organizing a party before Christmas and asked me if I were going to be there, which of course I confirmed.

At that time, I had my representative office with about ten employees, and I owned thirteen Benetton stores in the UK with 120 employees, between full- and part-timers. I couldn't miss the party.

In general, I have never liked showing off, and liked it even less when done by somebody else, but that time I thought, *Things are going well, our staff is working hard and so I will surprise them renting a nice Ferrari at the airport and then let them try the car around the block, to have some fun!*

So, I did it when I arrived at Heathrow; it was a very nice F355 brand new, red colour, with which I drove to Reading where my office was.

Then, thinking of giving them a surprise, I was myself surprised by the fact that the party, more than a Christmas' one, had been organized to celebrate my 100th flight in that year! I hadn't even imagined that it would be possible but that year I had taken, on average, a flight every four days! That's a lot, by anybody's standards.

At the end, we all had fun and the party was fantastic!

While living in Dubai, where I was from 1989 for fifteen years, I started to take flying lessons at the Emirates Flying school.

This is part of the International Dubai airport, and you take your lessons with instructors on either Piper or Cessna 172 among all the other commercial flights.

You should be able to take your license in six months, with 45 hours, but due to my business obligations, I didn't find the time to complete it.

However, I had reached the level of talking directly with the Control Tower and having a flight basically all by myself, although always with the instructor in the aircraft with me.

One day I was taxing to the assigned runaway for take-off, it was very hot, and the small air conditioning system was insufficient.

There is a small triangular window you can open to get extra fresh air, which I did.

We were slowly moving, when I had the strange feeling of being 'observed', I turned and behind me I had a huge Jumbo Boeing 747.

Now, think that my single-engine aircraft was 3 mt. tall, and the Jumbo was 20 mt. tall!

It was like walking with an elephant behind you!

I suddenly felt the urge to put my arm outside the window and wave the Jumbo through, as you do when you are in a slow car, and you want a Porsche or Ferrari overtake you and go ahead!

While my instructor, a nice Indian guy with no sense of humour, was screaming, "Are you crazy? You cannot do that, you must respect the order of take-off given by the Control Tower!" as I didn't know that, the two jumbo pilots were laughing and they gave me their thumbs up, of course understanding my joke!

It was truly a funny moment!

Another flying situation developed during a vacation with friends in Turks & Caicos, the beautiful Caribbean Islands.

We were four couples and our trip had to continue to Cuba after the first week in Turks.

Back in 1993 there was still the US embargo and therefore no direct flight to Havana. Our tickets were providing for a flight from Turks & Caicos to Miami, from there a connecting flight to Cancun, in Mexico, and finally from Cancun the only possible flight to Havana! A full day trip!

It was an absurd very long trip, and we had Santiago de Cuba at only a couple of hours flight away!

I then went to a local aeroclub, organizing tourist flights in the area, and asked if there was anybody ready to take us to Santiago.

A young local pilot immediately said yes and, after agreeing the price, we planned the trip for the following days.

He had an aircraft with two engines, a 12-seater, that he would be flying alone. (This was already an illegal provision, since a commercial flight must have two pilots, in case something happens to one!)

Anyway, we met and prepared to take-off, when I said to him "I'm taking flying lessons in Dubai and quite advanced, do you mind if I seat in front with you at the co-pilot position?"

He had no problem with that, and we left, with Chiara and the other four friends in the main cabin, separated from the cockpit only by a simple curtain.

We were flying at around 4,500 ft, and I was enjoying the flight and asking many questions on the instruments and details of the aircraft, from which the pilot understood that I was really knowledgeable about it.

Suddenly I told him, "Look, I would like to make a joke to my friends. If you put your hands joined together on top of your head, so that it visible that you are NOT flying the plane, and I start going up and down and left and right, they will go crazy!"

He was a little dubious for a few moments, and then smiled and said, "OK, let's do it, but you have to be very careful in going nose down, because this plane is dangerous in that situation, it goes rapidly very down!"

I reassured him, "Don't worry, I'll be very gentle, and you can be prompt to take the joystick back if you deem so."

A few moment later the plane was going everywhere and one of my friends shouted, "Francesco is piloting the plane, what the hell…?"

All the others, particularly the ladies, followed screaming in fear, with pieces of luggage falling from the side open storage, then I quickly stopped the movements, and we went back to straight flight, with me and the pilot laughing to each other and my friends swearing at me!

In the Middle East, by the end of 1999, we had reached 85 "United Colors of Benetton" points of sale, 55 of "012" (the children-wear line including newborn babies), and 30 "Sisley" for a total of $35 million at industrial cost, equivalent to approximately $100 million retail sales.

The 012 line of children-wear was representing roughly 50% of the total and it was by far the highest pro-capita in Benetton worldwide!

Even the domestic Italian market didn't reach these levels, and it is historically the best for children, given the inclination of Italian parents to spend for their children they want to be smartly dressed. This is the opposite of the British ones that don't care, as all that matters is to spend the minimum possible. "Children grow fast anyway, why throw away money?"

One day I was in Benetton in Italy for various meetings, I was suddenly notified that Gilberto's secretary was looking for me urgently.

From another internal office I called, and she said, "Francesco, I know this wasn't planned, but Gilberto would like to see you today, any time before you leave."

I answered, "Ok, I will be free around 5:30 pm. Does that fit?"

"Perfect," she said, "see you then."

It made me think. It was strange, Gilberto could not have any urgent reason to see me, my contacts with him were limited to administrative issues and there was, in my knowledge, nothing wrong with any of my clients in reference to payments or issue of letters of credit.

An urgent matter would have been possible with the Commercial Dept., not with Gilberto!

The more I thought, the less I was understanding the possible reason of such need to see me!

At 5:30 pm I got to his office, and we met. After the usual start talks, he began to look at a big stack of computer printed reports and, vaguely, to talk about the average order of "012" line in the stores.

He then referred to our area averages (the Middle East), underlying how they were much higher than the average.

I was initially pleased with this, thinking he was congratulating me for a good job done, but his serious face while he kept talking made me suddenly suspicious.

He continued highlighting the details of 'Zerotondo' (the newborn baby line), where the numbers were even more astonishing to him in relation to the number of points of sale in my area.

I suddenly understood and a moment later he said, "Francesco, are you sure your clients sell all this merchandise in their own stores?"

I couldn't refrain from laughing and I said, "Gilberto, are you thinking at some parallel market where these goods might go? I hope you do not intend that I do it on purpose, right?"

"No, no Francesco!" he said slightly embarrassed, "I fully trust you!

I just meant that, since these sales are incredibly high, maybe some of your clients do it behind your back somewhere else."

"I understand," I continued, "since you know little of our market (he had never been in the Middle East) it's obvious you can doubt that these are genuine orders sold in the stores, but let me tell you, if you asked Luciano, he has seen with me, various times, incredible shopping events in the stores that you would not believe if you didn't see with your own eyes! The population in the Middle East has an average age of 28 years compared to the average European one of 43!

There are therefore many kids, particularly since Arabs marry very young and they have easily four or five children at least!"

He was incredulously listening, and I continued, "And there is another incredible factor you would never guess: most of the rich Arab mothers, particularly the royal ones (and they are many!), don't wash the newborn clothes, they throw them away! They would never re-use some clothes were the infant has done his poo! They take a new one!

This by itself multiplies by... I don't even know how many times the equivalent spending of a European mother!

You must change a baby three times a day, and waiting for the next size, if you washed them, it could easily be a hundred and eighty outfits you use, instead of two or three!"

He could not believe what he was hearing, I then added "Luciano was with me in the Kuwait megastore during last Ramadan (the Holy period of fasting for the Muslims, when basically they sleep during the day and live during the night, imagine that Benetton stores were open until 2 am!). Well, there was a royal young princess, with the driver and another bodyguard assisting her (she would never, by the way, carry a shopping bag!), who spent more than $15,000 in two hours! That means nearly 400 garments for children! Can you imagine? Let me assure you, there is no parallel market, we are really selling these numbers in the Gulf, we are just lucky it's the way it is!"

He finally smiled and said, "I hope you are not upset for what I asked you, but even my management could not understand these figures! Now that you explained what happens, everything's clear and we must be happy about it! Maybe I should come one day with Luciano to your area, it must be very interesting to see."

I would have liked to welcome him in Dubai, but he never came.

16

Luciano, the Ram's Eye and the Tsar's Plate, Stinnes and the Oil By-products

D ubai, March 1996.
Luciano came to the Gulf countries for an official visit and arrived with his private jet, together with our common friend and great restaurateur Gino Santin, and with the Benetton Area manager for the Middle East, Paolo Vazzoler.

Gino Santin had been one of my best friends since 1982, when I met him in one of his restaurants in UK.

Gino opened in 1984 the "Santini" in Chelsea, London, which immediately became the top Italian restaurant, where all the best actors, politicians, industrialists were going for dinner.

Just to give you an idea, Frank Sinatra celebrated his 80th birthday there and Sarah Ferguson regards Gino as a father because he protected her during the most difficult time of her life.

Gino is probably the guy with the best sense of humour I ever met!

Paolo Vazzoler was a basketball player with the Benetton team from 1979 until 1991, except for a couple of seasons elsewhere.

He was loved by the Benetton supporters because of his courage and dedication to the team and they nicknamed him 'the Warrior'!

After retirement from basketball, having a university degree in economics, he started to work inside Benetton Group as a marketing manager and he was appointed new area manager of the MEMA, and since then we've been good friends.

In Dubai, waiting for them we had prepared some official meetings through our client, H.E. Easa Saleh Al Gurg and his favourite daughter, Raja, who was in charge of the Benetton division.

A successful businessman and diplomat (he was UAE ambassador in the UK at the time), Easa was a wise man that had used at perfection the best tool he had: he was one of the very few, if not the only one, to have studied and could be involved in the relationship with governments and politicians at the time of the sudden boom of the oil industry in the Gulf.

He became close friend of both the Emir of Dubai, Sheikh Rashid Al Maktoum, as well as the Emir of Abu Dhabi, Sheikh Zayed Al Nahyan.

As such, he was able to get many good exclusive distributorship agreements in different sectors and built his own empire.

One day we had a meeting just the two of us, and after having finished he said, "Francesco, why don't you leave that wife of yours (he didn't like my wife Chiara because she was often aggressive with his daughter Raja on the lack of image and good management in the stores, and quite rightly so!) become a Muslim and I will introduce you to a very good young Arab girl, from one of the best families in Dubai, for you to marry and then you'll be rich, happy and well respected?"

"Thank you, Mr. Easa," I said, "but I love my wife and wouldn't possibly leave her just for some opportunity of wealth and career."

"Well, think about it and we'll see. In the meantime, I want to give you a present but, will you make a promise to me?"

While I was trying to guess what he was talking about, I quickly answered, "If I can, Mr. Easa! I don't know what you want me to promise!"

He stood up and went towards the library at his back on the wall and picked a book. It was a Koran.

He then said, "I am going to give you this Holy Koran in English for you to read, but can you promise me that you'll never, ever touch it if that day you have drunk any alcohol?"

I immediately answered "Yes, of course, I promise you!" and I did it in good faith, knowing I was being honest since in reality, given that I adore wine and I drink it every day, I would have never touched the Koran! It was that simple.

I went back and told the story to my wife Chiara (who by the way was my third wife… I was almost as an Arab who could have had four of them, and even at the same time!) and emphasized the dedication the average Arab had to his religion, praying five times a day, not eating pork and not drinking wine, all in all much more coherent than Catholics.

We are not very devout; we don't go to church that much and we don't respect all the limitations imposed by our religion. In reality we are Catholics as a façade, but nothing else.

When we went to London next time, during the summer, I said to Chiara, "We must invite Mr. Easa and his wife for dinner, in return for all his invitations and homages. I will call him to arrange it and then I will alert my friend Gino."

I did so, we booked the table for four, I went personally to the restaurant to make sure we had the best possible table, away from the confusion and, above all, away from any alcohol!

"Please Gino, it's very important to me, your waiters must be very careful not to offer any alcoholic beverage, it would be a serious insult, he is a good Muslim and doesn't drink."

The night of the dinner came, we met at the restaurant Santini, we were introduced to his wife, whom I had never met yet, and then accompanied to our table.

Then the waiters arrived, as instructed, with orange juice, sparkling and still water, and I asked my guests what they would prefer.

Easa said, "Water? Oh no, thanks! I'll have a nice gin and tonic with Sapphire gin, please!"

We went on with a nice bottle of Super Tuscan Solaia and afterwards with a nice whisky.

Let's toast to coherence!

Anyway, let's go back to Luciano's visit.

After a meeting with some ministries of Dubai, we all had lunch in Mr. Easa's beautiful villa, with about twenty people there.

I was sitting as usual next to Luciano, to be able to translate, and to my left I had Paolo.

As main course a beautiful rice and mutton arrived on the table, with the full head in the middle, as tradition wants.

Gently, Mr. Easa took out one eye from the head and offered it to Luciano, with his hands, in sign of respect like the old Bedouins used to do when heads of tribes would meet.

Luciano promptly accepted and thanked his guest, taking the eye and then putting it on his plate.

They served him with rice and meat, and we all started to eat. It was delicious! Even Paolo on my left, who was usually very fussy with food (he would normally always eat the same things: pasta, bread, etc.), was really enjoying his lunch.

Suddenly however, with a sneer on his face, Luciano said, "Would you please pass this eye to Paolo? I know he loves it." And he gave me a small plate, on which he had placed the single eye.

I passed it on to Paolo, who had heard, and although he was really trying to do his best, felt that the entire room was looking at him, put it in his mouth but couldn't really swallow it and, almost suffocating, had to spit it out! Luckily Mr. Easa, followed by all the others, burst out laughing and that was it!

After lunch, Mr. Easa wanted proudly to show Mr. Luciano and us his living room, where he had on display various plates apparently of great value.

We went on taking these plates in our hands, pretending to admire them, until we came to a corner unit that had a full set of plates.

Mr. Easa took one out a gave it to Luciano saying, "These are coming from a private collection of Russian Tsar Alexander III, back in the nineteenth century."

The plate went carefully around to me and then to Gino. While Easa was pompously describing something on the collection, Gino turned the back of the plate upside down and said loudly "Oh, look here, there is still the Harrod's sticker with the price!"

It wasn't true, there was no sticker, Gino just wanted to see Easa's reaction and as expected, Easa took the plate from his hands abruptly and screamed, "No, they didn't!" confirming that the plates were not at all coming from an auction of the Tsar's property!

Afterwards, in the hotel, the four of us kept laughing into tears just thinking at Mr. Easa's face.

The following day we had dinner in Dubai at Casa Mia, the Italian restaurant at the Meridien Hotel, run by our friends Maurizio and Patrizia Lazzarin, in my view the only true Italian food in Dubai, at that time.

We were having a nice and relaxed general conversation and drinking a fine Barolo of 'Borgogno', one of the best old labels in Piemonte.

I love the very mature Barolo, the only Italian wine that can really age well, like the top French Bordeaux and Bourgogne, and that bottle, in my view, was a waste, since it was a 1990 vintage.

The 1990 was a great vintage for all regions and in my view would have been perfect to drink in at least another six to eight years, but my friend Gino Santin, a great restaurateur in London and Milan, didn't agree.

Gino didn't like old wines and, once again, a discussion started on the subject, with Luciano as an amused witness, since he didn't really bother with wines.

He was enjoying a glass of wine, not more, at dinner, but he didn't really know anything of the incredible world of this fantastic drink that has pleased the tables in centuries of history.

The discussion became a bit heated, since I was claiming the beauty of a 1964 or, even better, a 1971 Barolo, with funny accusations on my side regarding Gino's supposed 'ignorance', inexcusable in his professional position, "And that was revealing is humble origin of a countryside person grown around Jesolo, where only money and screwing the tourists would count!"

It was normal for us to jokingly fight on issues, insulting each other in a way that was only understandable to us, the others would think that we were really fighting and afraid that the discussion would degenerate!

But it never did, it was our peculiar way to have fun.

Luciano knew both of us too well not to know that this was a game, but our tablemates started to look worried, until Gino came up with a comment that still makes me crying laugh these days, "Listen, drinking a 40-year-old Barolo is like having a beautiful 25-year-old woman, locking her in the tower of a medieval castle and going back to have sex with her when she is 70!"

There was an explosion of laughs and that ended the subject, with me admitting that, put in this way, he was crystal clear, and I couldn't agree more!

In the same period, I had a meeting in Geneva, with a banker friend of mine, and he asked me, since we were having lunch at the Bank (they had a very good chef and some private rooms for their guests' lunch), if he could introduce to me a young German manager of Stinnes AG, the German industrial giant trading, among other, oil by-products.

He explained to me that the market of by-products was controlled by an international cartel and that Stinnes had been trying to buy oil by-products from ADNOC (Abu Dhabi National Oil Company) since a few years and never succeeded. It was a very simple, official request of buying a product but, for some reason, it never happened.

He concluded that probably the matter needed some 'push' from inside and asked me if I had any good contact in this direction and stated that, of course, there would have been a substantial commission included in the deal, that I could use in part to compensate the 'push' and the rest for me.

I answered that I knew someone and would try.

Upon my return to Dubai, I met with an Arab good friend of mine who was in a high position with the Government of Dubai, working closely with Sheik Mohammed and had obviously contacts in Abu Dhabi.

I explained the deal and that we had an opportunity to make a lot of money, everything in an official way, it was just a matter of getting ADNOC to supply Stinnes AG.

We then had a very private meeting in Abu Dhabi with two high ranking managers of ADNOC who were very evasive during the meeting, but on our way back to Dubai my friend was overall optimistic.

A couple of days later I was in my office in Dubai when my telephone rang, it was my secretary who said, "Francesco, there is a guy, I believe Arab, who is asking to talk to you about the ADNOC deal? I don't know anything about this, so I put him on hold…" (Of course, she didn't know anything about this, it was very private and I kept it secret…).

I said, "Pass me the call."

A deep voice, with strong Arab accent, said to me in a rough English "Mr. Francesco, you are selling Benetton T-shirts since many years ago, and you have two beautiful daughters in Milan, Eleonora and Simona…" and he continued telling me where they were going to school, who was the baby sitter helping my ex-wife, and while I was astonished and silent, he concluded, "You don't want anything to happen to your daughters, right? So, continue to sell T-shirts and forget ADNOC!" and hung up.

I remained for some time like frozen, asking myself if this was true or a nightmare, then I frenetically called my friend and, when he heard what happened, he immediately told me "Francesco, let's immediately drop the issue of ADNOC, we have touched a very sensitive issue and it's not our world, we better forget it!"

Of course, I followed his suggestion, informed the Stinnes' guy of it, and never again talked about it!

17

Arabs, Benetton and Sex; A Syrian Licensee and the End of the Market in the Middle East

When we started with Benetton back in 1981, the Arab countries were very underdeveloped and relatively poor, except for Bahrain, the most sophisticated one, and Kuwait.

In 1989 we decided to open our office in Dubai and Chiara, who had an important experience in the fashion business with brands like Armani, Ralph Lauren, and others, joined me as a partner and has taken care of the 'fashion' side of our business for thirty years, while I was more in marketing and financing.

Looking backwards, I must say that we have not been just a great couple in life, but also in our work. We have always been able to take care of our own responsibilities without interfering between us, and this was possible because we had the absolute trust and certainty that the other would do his job with the best dedication and professionalism. This is why Chiara was so esteemed and regarded as an expert by all our clients and even by all the various Benetton departments.

One of the first great moments was when, with Luciano, we announced the opening of the new office and the future plans of development of our brand in the Middle East, with a press conference in Dubai.

There was no Western fashion brand, Benetton was by far the first one to develop a proper presence in the area.

Saudi Arabia was the richest and potentially the best market for us, but we had several limitations and obstacles.

Women: Saudi women were not allowed to dress Western clothes in public, they had to cover themselves with the *abaya*, that black 'dress' that most people think is a real dress, instead it's only a cover, under which they wear all the most expensive fashion brands, name it.

In addition, women could not work, drive the car, or any other role that would bring them in touch with a man, except for their husbands.

This was a contradiction in terms, or a 'catch 22' as they say in US: since women could not work, in fashion stores you only found male sales-assistants who, however, in turn were talking to customers that were 90 % female, and these women shouldn't have talked or, even worse, been seen in their face by such males!

Materials: all our promotional materials, such as window displays and photo panels, mannequins, and other advertising things, were illegal.

All this, once again, for the same basic reason that showing any part of the body in public was not acceptable, whether male or female.

Any fashion shows that we might want to organize, was also not permitted, so basically no communication was there to promote your new fashion trends and, when you think that Internet had still to come, you have a pretty good idea!

Even the most innocent prints of kitties and puppies had to be removed from the collection because they would be regarded as impure.

As a matter of fact, you could find any sort of alcohol and drugs in the country, even if for drugs there was death penalty for possession of such elements!

And you would find this warning, printed in red, in the immigration form at your arrival in any Saudi airport.

So, how was it possible? The only people that could bring into the country a container without going through the meticulous screening of Customs agents, were the royal princes. You take the conclusion.

In this abnormal scenario, the most intricated stories of sex and drugs took place. You wonder, how was it possible if women were so strictly controlled? There is an explanation for everything.

For instance, a Saudi wealthy husband would want to be certain that his young and beautiful wife could not be approachable by anybody!

Therefore, her private driver, to carry her around anywhere by car, very often was a eunuch.

Saudis would go to poor African countries, like Sudan, to buy small children in numbers, bring them to Saudi, castrate them and then make them become either drivers, loyal to their owner / employer, or camel jockeys.

So, let's say he had to go away until the evening, he would give his wife a stack of cash, literally a roll of banknotes equivalent to thousands of dollars, for her shopping.

And here the unthinkable would happen:

Imagine the wife had seen at a shopping centre, a young and attractive guy she would like to see.

She would walk up and down the corridor with a girlfriend of her, having written her mobile number on the palm. She would make sure he had a glance at the number, and then talk to him over the phone, until a relationship had started.

At that point, whenever she had decided to have finally sex with the guy, she would go, once again, with her girlfriend for shopping and would instruct the driver to wait for them three hours later in the lower-level parking of the centre.

She would then leave all the cash with her accomplice friend who would casually spend it all in the next three hours.

In the meantime, she would meet with the lover, go with him to his apartment, have sex and then go back in time to meet her friend, and finally return home, with plenty of shopping bags for her and the children.

This is a true story, not an imagination or fiction!

And another one, even more incredible:

A young handsome Egyptian guy was working in a Benetton store in Jeddah.

As usual, when the prayer time came (in Islam it's five times a day, so the second one is normally around lunch time), the staff had to ask all customers to leave the store and lock it.

One day he saw a female customer still looking for something in the children area, out of the view from the entrance, and went there asking respectfully the lady to leave for the prayer.

She turned and, without saying anything, she opened her abaya, and she was only with panties on, almost naked.

He was shocked, both for the beauty of the young girl

and for the danger of the situation, they could have been both executed if found.

He quickly rushed back to the entrance, and she calmly left without a word.

After a few days, the scene repeated the same way, and then again until the guy could not resist any more, he met secretly the girl outside and they became lovers.

The secret relationship went on for a while, until one day he received a call by her in the store and she told him,

"In two hours, I will send my driver to pick up a girl friend of mine at the so-and-so hotel, and that girl is going to be you!"

"Are you crazy?" he answered. "How can I pretend to be a woman and why should I come to your home?!"

She explained, "If you fully dress like a woman, with high heels, all covered, nobody can imagine you are a man, you just stay silent, and he will drive you to my place.

"When you arrive, I'll be there waiting for you. We'll go to the ladies' quarter and leave our shoes out, as it is tradition (it's really like that, to prevent that accidentally any male, a servant or the husband or brother, saw a friend in the face, it is a signal that, if ladies' shoes are left outside the door entrance to the ladies' room, it means the wife is inside with one or more friends and no male can go in).

"In that way nobody will dare coming in, not even my husband, who anyway is on a trip to Riyadh and will only come back tomorrow. I desperately want to make love to you, do you understand?"

I heard this story when the guy called me in Dubai, very nervous, almost desperate, to ask for my help to quickly get him out of the country.

I listened to the story, then I asked him, "Did you really make love there in her own palace?"

He said, "Yes, yes! It's crazy, I know, but it was so exciting I couldn't resist, and it was fantastic!"

"But now," he continued, "she has become very possessive and jealous and is threatening me that, if I don't do everything she asks me, she will tell her husband about me! If that happens, he will get me cut into pieces and throw them away in the desert! Please, help me, can you get me immediately a job in Dubai? I will accept any condition, please!"

He was almost crying with fear, and so I did arrange as soon as I could for him to escape to Dubai. What a story!

But the moral is that her husband deserved to be cheated! When you treat your wife without any trust, and you only control her as strictly as possible, you can only get, in the long run, such a reaction in revenge!

In those days, even when Luciano was coming to Saudi on an official trip, it was very difficult for Chiara to get a visa, still the Saudis didn't like women coming to their country for business reasons, probably because it was inducing some of their women to think that they would want to do the same.

Me and Chiara eventually got married in 1993, in Marlow in UK, with a wonderful ceremony involving only thirty of our best friends and relatives, during a weekend with a lot of fun and unforgettable moments.

But it was not reported yet on our Italian passports during our trip with Luciano to Saudi and so, with our surprise, at the hotel in Jeddah they said to us that we had to sleep in different rooms, on different floors, because we were considered as 'singles'!

We took it in a spirit of fun. I thought, "It will be even more romantic and exciting to sneak into her room tonight!"

Which I did, carefully making sure not to be seen, taking the elevator to her floor, and knocking with an agreed 'code' on her door.

We were happily sleeping, a couple of hours later, when the room telephone rang on her side, and I heard her saying something like, "Who is this? What do you want?"

I turned the light on and asked what the hell was going on and, with a sleepy face, she told me, "There is a man who is proposing to come up and have sex with me!"

I picked up the phone and surprised him (he didn't expect to find a man on the other side) and told him to go away or come up and I would break his face! He hung up and that was it!

Typically, a Saudi man that, having seen a beautiful foreign woman in the hotel, thought she was like a prostitute and therefore available for money and, probably knowing someone in the hotel, had been able to get her room number and try to reach his objective!

So, every day in Saudi was an adventure, you never knew what could happen next, like that time when, during another trip with Luciano, we were coming out of a Benetton store in Jeddah, in an open new beautiful mall, where Chiara had been very busy to show their staff, in presence of Luciano, how to prepare a window and to accordingly merchandise the store to reflect what the new collection wanted to emphasize.

We went outside and she forgot, being busy to explain something to Luciano, to cover her head and hair with the veil that all women use.

Chiara knew very well how to move around in a Muslim community, always properly dressed not to create any embarrassment, or worse, complaint, but that day, in the excitement of the situation, she forgot!

We didn't notice that a *mutawa* was arriving behind us. The *mutawa* were religious individuals escorted by armed officers of the local police, that were considered like 'religious police' and were enforcing, if necessary, the respect of Muslim rules in public. They were normally carrying a bamboo stick and this guy, seeing Chiara with her veil on her shoulders instead that covering her head, hit her sharply with the stick on a shoulder! She screamed in pain, I suddenly turned and realized what was happening and launched myself on the guy to beat him!

Luckily, a couple of Saudi guys working with our local client jumped on me and stopped me, otherwise I would have been probably beaten by the two police officers and arrested. And you don't want to spend even one hour in a Saudi prison...

Later there was a gala dinner organized in honour of Luciano, with 40 people attending in a beautiful palace's garden, with all the "Mezzeh" appetizers on the big table.

We were sitting in the middle, I had Luciano at my right and in front of us a minister of Jeddah, of the Al Saud royal family, and Abdul Khader.

It was really a wonderful dinner; the food was extraordinary, and I was only missing... a good glass of wine! (In respect of the Muslim religion there was, of course, no alcohol on the table).

We had heard in the afternoon that peace negotiations between Barak and Arafat, under the influence of Bill Clinton, were going well and that a final peace agreement between Israel, Palestine and other Arab countries would have soon been reached, bringing, perhaps, a period of long-term peace and prosperity to the region.

Luciano, therefore, decided to say a few words to celebrate this moment and asked me, as usual, to play the interpreter's role, translating his Italian speech into English.

As soon as he finished, thinking probably to receive a round of applause, we instead heard what Abdul Khader had to say, still eating his food, "Tell Mr. Luciano that in the Holy Koran is written that we will only be capable of being happy and live in peace when the last of the Jews on Earth will be dead!"

We were frozen having heard the asperity of his speech, the hater against Israel behind it and so we decided to shut up, enjoy the rest of the evening and never talk again about political issues!

In 2001 we moved our office to Beirut, in Lebanon, where I joined Tony Zaatar, a client and representative of Benetton for Beirut.

We created a new and beautiful Benetton representative office for all the Middle East, more than 5,000 sq. ft. of space, that included also Beirut and Syria, before controlled only by Tony.

Syria was a particular situation. I had met the Syrian owner of a local factory of garments who had obtained, through Tony's introduction and negotiation, a Manufacturing License from Benetton Group .

Basically, he was receiving the models from Benetton and was producing in his factory all the classic styles, with a very good cotton and fabrication quality, for the Benetton stores in Syria and Lebanon.

I was surprised by the overall quality of these garments, particularly in terms of price/quality ratio.

The sales results in Lebanon were excellent, with a pre-end-of-season sale of very high percentage.

I convinced myself that we needed to test these items in the rest of the Middle East, and soon.

Our stores had gone from incredible sales at the beginning, when we had been the first brand by far in the market, gradually to insufficient sales to guarantee e good return.

This was due essentially to the arrival of many new competitive brands such as Zara, Mango, Giordano and so on. They had taken away our business and suddenly our owners were complaining about budgets too high, not profitable performance, and so on.

I was living in a nightmare: I had already gone through this exact experience in USA ten years before and I was afraid that Benetton would make the same mistake.

But then I said to myself, "Come on, it is not possible that Luciano and everybody else in the company have not learnt the lesson, now they will welcome a solution to 'make Benetton great again' using a well know slogan of these days…"

I organized a meeting with Luciano, where I went with Tony and all the samples, sell-out data, and anything else needed to justify the necessary strategy: allow all the Benetton stores to buy freely from Syria at much cheaper prices and much better margins the 80% of their orders, with the other 20% form the so-called fashion selection made in Italy.

As icing on the cake, I had negotiated an incredible royalty fee payable to Benetton Group by the Syrian licensee: instead of the usual 6% on industrial sales, I had convinced him, in order to get the ok from Italy, to pay a stunning 15% royalty!

Unbelievably, history repeated itself, once again, and Luciano said no to us, refusing to allow the only way out of a deepening crisis.

I left the meeting completely exhausted, and after a few days of thinking, I went back to Luciano and said to him:

"I am sorry, Mr. Luciano, but after twenty-seven years of working with Benetton I must confess that I do not agree with the marketing strategy anymore. In these circumstances, I do not feel that I am the right person to represent you in the Middle East, because I would not be able to promote your business in a convincing manner. I could only continue to comfortably collect still important commissions, like any other of my colleagues' representatives would do, but in honesty I can only give you my resignation and invite you to find a better candidate for my position."

With my surprise Luciano was almost offended by my attitude, which I regarded as the only honest one, and told me "Francesco, I think you are not grateful to what Benetton has always done for you and all the agents. You should appreciate all the efforts we made for the success of our brand and the people involved with us.

Anyway, I take your decision and I will inform our people to do the necessary to define your departure as agent."

18

The End of the Love Affair

It was the 11th of September 2001, we were in our offices in Dubai at almost 6 pm in the afternoon, close to the point of leaving the office, when suddenly our secretary, who was looking at the Internet from the main office's computer, screamed and covered her face with her hands, and started crying!

We all ran to her, and we saw what will be remembered as one of the darkest days of mankind, the attack to the twin towers in NYC.

I had already grown tired of the Arab world, given the changes that took place in those years and forever compromised relationship between us and the Muslims.

When I started in 1981 to go to the middle east, Muslims were relaxed and hospitable despite our religious and social differences, which we were mutually respecting. They would offer you a cup of tea, even in the bazaars and more traditional places, treating you as a normal person, not an 'infidel'.

With the years going by, this attitude changed dramatically, deepening the differences between us and them, and the hostility became touchable, with physical difference as well.

That day we left the office, after calling around the world and receiving confirmation on the twin towers collapse and dreadful massive number of innocent lives taken away.

We went outside only to discover that, everywhere in Dubai, people had formed groups celebrating the terrorist attack and burning American flags in the middle of the street, jumping in happy and enthusiastic groups chanting against USA!

That's when I thought I had enough, I could no longer accept the anger against the Western countries and the general definition of a foreign citizen as an 'infidel' and, as such, to be rejected and even eliminated, in the name of Allah!

As I write these last few words, I think about the great man: Luciano Benetton, a smart guy that built an empire from nothing and has made, on the way, many people like me wealthy and successful.

We saw him a couple of years ago when he invited Chiara and me for lunch at his internal, very good restaurant for managers at his head-quarter, Villa Minelli.

We shared fond memories, had fun, and enjoyed each other's company.

Right before leaving, Chiara told him "Signor Luciano, mi lasci dire che lei è sempre un gran bel figo!" (Mr. Luciano, let me say that you are always a very handsome man!)

He had one of his famous smiles, while enjoying the compliment, and gave her a big hug!

And so, we said goodbye to each other, knowing we had been part of a very innovative age, full of achievements and of creative energy.

On our side, we will always be grateful to Luciano Benetton and his company for having given us the opportunity of living an extraordinary life.

Milton Keynes UK
Ingram Content Group UK Ltd.
UKHW020639160924
1€59UKWH00018B/35

9 781914 158124